THE AUTHOR: Takeo Doi, M.D., is a professor at International Christian University, Tokyo, and one of Japan's leading psychiatrists. Born in Tokyo, he graduated from the University of Tokyo in 1942. He has since held a number of posts at American institutes and universities, including fellowships at the Menninger School of Psychiatry and the San Francisco Psychoanalytic Institute, and was visiting scientist at the National Institute of Mental Health, Bethesda, Maryland. For a long time he headed the psychiatric department at St. Luke's International Hospital in Tokyo, and was also a professor in the schools of Health Science and Medicine at the University of Tokyo. Doi has published a number of works and contributed to many more. His most recent English publication is *The Anatomy of Self* (Kodansha International, 1985).

D0465493

The anatomy of dependence

Takeo Doi, M.D.

translated by
John Bester

KODANSHA INTERNATIONAL
Tokyo and New York

First published in 1971 under the title *Amae no Kōzō* by Kōbundō Ltd., Tokyo.

Distributed in the United States by Kodansha International/USA Ltd., 114 Fifth Avenue, New York, New York 10011. Published by Kodansha International Ltd., 17-14 Otowa 1-chome, Bunkyo-ku, Tokyo 112 and Kodansha International/USA Ltd. Copyright © 1973 by Kodansha International Ltd. All rights reserved. Printed in Japan.

LCC 81-85342
ISBN 0-87011-494-8
ISBN 4-7700-0979-8 (in Japan)

First edition, 1973
Revised paperback edition, 1981
Tenth printing, 1990

Contents

Note: Chapter 6 was added in 1981.

Foreword

To those specialists in the West who already know Dr. Doi's work, any foreword by a layman is unnecessary, if not impertinent. For other laymen, however, especially those who have not lived in Japan, a few preliminary words of explanation concerning the central concept of *amae* may be useful.

The original work translated here—*Amae no Kōzō*, literally "the structure of *amae*"—was written for the Japanese reader, for whom *amae* is part of his very fiber. For the Western reader, however, this central concept of *amae* is unfamiliar, and it is essential that at an early stage in his reading he should get something of the feel of it. Otherwise, it may remain for him a purely intellectual exercise, neither especially helpful in understanding the Japanese nor particularly relevant to his own experience. This would be a pity; for this work is, above all, about the felt reality of the Japanese experience—one of many different but equally valid human experiences, a knowledge of which cannot but illuminate and deepen our own.

The Japanese term *amae* refers, initially, to the feelings that all normal infants at the breast harbor toward the mother— dependence, the desire to be passively loved, the unwillingness to be separated from the warm mother-child circle and cast into a world of objective "reality." It is Dr. Doi's basic premise that in a Japanese these feelings are somehow prolonged into and diffused throughout his adult life, so that they come to shape, to a far greater extent than in adults in the West, his whole attitude to other people and to "reality."

On the personal level, this means that within his own most intimate circle, and to diminishing degrees outside that circle, he seeks relationships that, however binding they may be in their outward aspects, allow him to presume, as it were, on familiarity. For him, the assurance of another person's good will permits a certain degree of self-indulgence, and a corresponding degree of indifference to the claims of the other person as a separate individual. Such a relationship implies a considerable blurring of the distinction between subject and object; as such, it is not necessarily governed by what might be considered strict rational or moral standards, and may often seem selfish to the outsider. Sometimes even, the individual may deliberately act in a way that is "childish" as a sign to the other that he (in fact, as Dr. Doi points out, this is a license traditionally permitted among adults to women rather than men) wishes to be dependent and seeks the other's "indulgence."

It is the behavior of the child who desires spiritually to "snuggle up" to the mother, to be enveloped in an indulgent love, that is referred to in Japanese as *amaeru* (the verb; *amae* is the noun). By extension, it refers to the same behavior, whether unconscious or deliberately adopted, in the adult. And by extension again, it refers to any situation in which a person assumes that he has another's goodwill, or takes a—possibly unjustifiably—optimistic view of a particular situation in order to gratify his need to feel at one with, or indulged by, his surroundings.

Dr. Doi's primary aim here is to examine the implications of the existence in the Japanese language of a single word summing up this attitude, and of a whole vocabulary of related words that express what happens when *amae* is in some way or other frustrated or distorted. And he shows how the ramifications of the same basic mentality extend throughout the whole life of the individual and society in Japan. It is obvious, for

8

example, that where *amae* is so important to the individual the organization of society as a whole will take corresponding account of the individual's needs. To the insider, this thoughtfulness of society will seem particularly warm and "human"; to the outsider, it may seem to encourage self-indulgence and subjectivity. It is certainly true that, as Dr. Doi points out, the attempt always to remain warmly wrapped in one's own environment must to some extent involve a denial of reality, so that the claims of "objectivity" and "logic" are sometimes ignored.

The same carefully renewed sense—illusion, perhaps—of being at one with the outside world will also foster a peculiar passivity of outlook—a reluctance to do anything, whether in personal relationships or in society, that might disrupt the comfortable tenor of life, a reluctance to carry rationalism to the point where it will make the individual too aware of his separateness in relation to people and things about him. (An apparently violently disruptive act such as suicide can be seen, of course, simply as a retreat into a generalized *amae* as a result of some failure of localized *amae*.)

One could go on tracing the influence of the *amae* outlook almost indefinitely; to awaken to the significance of *amae* is to be given a key to a new understanding of the whole of Japanese society, culture, and art. What seems most important to me is that, where others have succeeded in describing the characteristic patterns of Japanese society, Dr. Doi succeeds—once one can feel what is meant by *amae*—in explaining them. To myself at least, his "key concept" has borne out and clarified all that I have observed during a long stay in Japan—and for the first time resolved the contradictions. Only a mentality rooted in *amae* could produce a people at once so unrealistic yet so clearsighted as to the basic human condition; so compassionate and so self-centered; so spiritual and so materialistic; so forbearing and so wilful; so docile and so violent—a people, in short, that

9

from its own point of view is preeminently normal and human in every respect.

This alone would make *The Anatomy of Dependence* an important book. But to explain the Japanese is only half the author's aim. Just as *amae* in the Japanese is of course tempered by various other characteristics superficially associated with the West, such as personal freedom, objectivity, and so on, so *amae* is an essential part of the humanity of Western man also. Just as the value attached to *amae* has accounted for both the virtues and the failings of Japanese society, so its suppression, or diversion into different channels, explains much of what is most admirable and detestable in the Western tradition. As Dr. Doi sees it, the basic human need summed up in the one Japanese word *amae* has been strangely neglected by Western psychologists and psychiatrists. This neglect has already been partly remedied by Dr. Doi's earlier work, and *The Anatomy of Dependence* should carry the good work farther. But any ordinary reader with an open mind should also find it fascinating for the light it throws not only on Japanese society but on his own as well. Wherever man builds up a society he is obliged afresh to allot relative importance to the various unchanging elements that make up his own animal nature, and to reconcile them with the whole. *The Anatomy of Dependence* shows how one unique and relatively isolated people set about that task.

JOHN BESTER

1 The first idea of *amae*

First, I should say something of how I originally became preoccupied with the concept of *amae*. It is related to my experience of what is generally referred to as "cultural shock." In 1950, I went to America on a GARIOA scholarship to study psychiatry. It was still not long after the end of the war, yet I was dazzled by the material affluence of America and impressed by the cheerful, uninhibited behavior of its people.

Nevertheless, from time to time I began to feel an awkwardness arising from the difference between my ways of thinking and feeling and those of my hosts. For example, not long after my arrival in America I visited the house of someone to whom I had been introduced by a Japanese acquaintance, and was talking to him when he asked me, "Are you hungry? We have some ice cream if you'd like it." As I remember, I was rather hungry, but finding myself asked point-blank if I was hungry by someone whom I was visiting for the first time, I could not bring myself to admit it, and ended by denying the suggestion. I probably cherished a mild hope that he would press me again; but my host, disappointingly, said "I see" with no further ado, leaving me regretting that I had not replied more honestly. And I found myself thinking that a Japanese would almost never ask a stranger unceremoniously if he was hungry, but would produce something to give him without asking.

Another case happened—also, as I remember, during my early days in America—when a psychiatrist who was my supervisor did me some kindness or other—I have forgotten exactly what, but it was something quite trivial. Either way, feeling the need to say something, I produced not "thank you," as one might expect, but "I'm sorry." "What are you sorry for?" he replied promptly, giving me an odd look. I was highly embarrassed. My difficulty in saying "thank you" arose, I imagine, from a feeling that it implied too great an equality with someone who was in fact my superior. In Japanese, I suppose, I should have said *dōmo arigatō gozaimasu* or *dōmo sumimasen*, but, unable to express the same feeling of obligation in English, I had come up with "I am sorry" as the nearest equivalent. The reason, of course, was undoubtedly my deficiency in English at the time. But I had already begun to have an inkling that the difficulty I faced involved something more than the language barrier.

Another thing that made me nervous was the custom whereby an American host will ask a guest, before the meal, whether he would prefer a strong or a soft drink. Then, if the guest asks for liquor, he will ask him whether, for example, he prefers scotch or bourbon. When the guest has made this decision, he next has to give instructions as to how much he wishes to drink, and how he wants it served. With the main meal, fortunately, one has only to eat what one is served, but once it is over one has to choose whether to take coffee or tea, and—in even greater detail—whether one wants it with sugar, and milk, and so on. I soon realized that this was only the American's way of showing politeness to his guest, but in my own mind I had a strong feeling that I couldn't care less. What a lot of trivial choices they were obliging one to make—I sometimes felt—almost as though they were doing it to reassure themselves of their own freedom. My perplexity, of course, undoubtedly came from my unfamiliarity with American social customs, and I would perhaps have done better to accept it as it stood, as an American custom.

Nor is it true, even, that the Japanese never ask a guest his preference. Nevertheless, a Japanese has to be very intimate with a guest before he will ask him whether he likes something he offers him. The custom, rather, in serving a guest who is not such a close friend is to produce something with a deprecatory "it may not suit your taste but . . ." An American hostess, on the other hand, will sometimes proudly describe how she made the main dish, which she produces without offering any alternative even as she gives her guests freedom of choice concerning the drinks that precede or follow it. This struck me as very odd indeed.

In this connection, the "please help yourself" that Americans use so often had a rather unpleasant ring in my ears before I became used to English conversation. The meaning, of course, is simply "please take what you want without hesitation," but literally translated it has somehow a flavor of "nobody else will help you," and I could not see how it came to be an expression of good will. The Japanese sensibility would demand that, in entertaining, a host should show sensitivity in detecting what was required and should himself "help" his guests. To leave a guest unfamiliar with the house to "help himself" would seem excessively lacking in consideration. This increased still further my feeling that Americans were a people who did not show the same consideration and sensitivity towards others as the Japanese. As a result, my early days in America, which would have been lonely at any rate, so far from home, were made lonelier still.

It was around this time that an American lady I got to know lent me Ruth Benedict's *The Chrysanthemum and the Sword*.[1] I read it immediately, and I still remember the vivid impression I had of seeing myself reflected in it. Time and again, as I turned the pages, I gave a nod of surprised recognition. At the same time the book stirred my intellectual curiosity as to why the Japanese and the Americans should be so different.

13

Perhaps because of the experiences I have just related, when I returned to Japan in 1952 I began to use my own eyes and ears in the attempt to discover just what it was that made the Japanese what they were. All the while I was attending to patients, I was asking myself how they differed from American patients. I paid careful attention to the words they used to describe their own condition and racked my brains as to how to set them down accurately in Japanese.

This may seem an obvious thing for a psychiatrist to do, but in fact it was not so obvious, since it had traditionally been the practice for Japanese doctors to listen to their patients and take down essential points in a very restricted number of German words. In the hands of Japanese doctors, the most ordinary everyday German words were treated almost as scientific terms; and anything that would not go into German had naturally to be discarded. This same trend was not, in fact, limited to psychiatry but was to be found in other specialist fields as well, and I had always thought it odd. When I went to America I found, of course, that psychiatrists there recorded what their patients said in their own language and that they pursued their consideration of their patients' pathology in their own tongues. Convinced that this was the only proper way, I determined that so long as I was examining Japanese patients I would record things and think about things in Japanese.

As I put these principles into practice, it was borne in on me that if there was anything unique about the Japanese psychology it must be closely related with the uniqueness of the Japanese language. It happened that in 1954 I was asked to give an outline account of psychiatry in Japan at a conference of U. S. military psychiatrists held in Tokyo. Towards the end of the lecture[2] I said in essence what follows: Attempts have been made to elucidate the peculiar nature of the Japanese psychology using projective tests, but, even if such methods produce results of a kind, I cannot believe that they will give a grasp of

14

the most Japanese characteristics of all, since the types of Japanese characteristics that can be detected by psychological tests designed for Westerners are, ultimately, Japanese characteristics as seen through Western eyes; the tests cannot overcome this limitation. "The typical psychology of a given nation can be learned only through familiarity with its native language. The language comprises everything which is intrinsic to the soul of a nation and therefore provides the best projective test there is for each nation."

I cannot clearly recall now just how aware I was, at the time I gave this lecture, of the unique implications of the word *amaeru*. But it is certain that something was already brewing in my mind as a result of my observations of large numbers of patients. I was in the psychiatry department of the Tokyo University School of Medicine at the time, and I remember one day, in a conversation with Professor Uchimura Yushi, head of the department, remarking that the concept of *amaeru* seemed to be peculiar to the Japanese language. "I wonder, though—" he said. "Why, even a puppy does it." The inference was that it was impossible that a word describing a phenomenon so universal that it was to be found not only among human beings but even among animals should exist in Japanese but not in other languages. I myself thought, however, that it was precisely this that made the fact so important. And my private conviction grew deeper that the special qualities of the Japanese psychology had a close relationship with this fact.

In 1955, I went to America again, where at an assembly of American psychiatrists on the West Coast I read a paper on "The Japanese Language and Psychology"[3] in which I set forth the ideas that were fermenting in my head. I began with a discussion of the relationship between language and psychology, then went on to explain the psychology of *amae* and the meaning of various apparently related terms, as well as the concept of *ki*.

While the aim of this paper, of course, was to elucidate the peculiar qualities of the Japanese psychology, it was also, in fact, to serve as a basis for all my subsequent psychological studies. A few days after the conference, I was surprised to receive an invitation from Dr. Frieda Fromm-Reichmann, well known for the psychotherapy of schizophrenia. She was at the Center at Palo Alto that year, and suggested I should visit her there and present my ideas to the other research workers. I was highly delighted that such an outstanding psychiatrist, and one, moreover, who had not made a special study of the Japanese psychology, should have shown an interest in my paper. I went to see her without delay and found she was particularly interested by the concept of *amaeru* and the concept of *ki*. She had perceived that the word *amaeru* suggested an affirmative attitude toward the spirit of dependence on the part of the Japanese. She also pointed out that the impersonal use of *ki* had some resemblance to the characteristic speech of schizophrenics. Among the small group who heard my talk at the Center was Dr. Hayakawa, the semanticist who subsequently, as president of San Francisco State College, made a name for himself by his handling of student disturbances there. A Canadian-born Nisei, he knows almost no Japanese, and was ignorant of all the terms I cited. Even so, I found it extremely interesting when he asked me if the feeling of *amaeru* was similar to that experienced by a Catholic towards the Blessed Virgin.

Shortly after this, I wrote my first short essay[4] on *amae* in Japanese. At the very beginning of it, I quoted the following short passage from Osaragi Jirō's novel *Homecoming*: "That's typical of the Japanese—they feel that if someone's a relative it gives them the right to presume on them (*amaeru*) or harbor emotional resentments just as they like. That's what I don't like. I hope I've grown out of that, at least. What difference is there, really, between relatives and the stranger next door?"

I read the book at the recommendation of Professor Itō

Kiyoshi, a mathematician whom I got to know at International House in Berkeley, and my sympathy for the chief character Kyōgo seems to have been all the stronger in that I myself happened, at the time I came across it, to be in alien surroundings and preoccupied with the question of *amae*. I accordingly added the following comment: "The emotion felt here by the work's hero, who has lived many years abroad is, I suspect, something that would only be experienced by someone who had spent some time in other countries."

I had come to realize that something had changed in myself as a result of the "cultural shock" I suffered when I first went to America. I came back to Japan with a new sensibility, and from then on the chief characteristic of the Japanese in my eyes was something that—as Kyōgo, the hero of *Homecoming*, also felt—could best be expressed by the word *amae*.

On my return from my second visit to America I set about using my idea that *amae* might be vitally important in understanding the Japanese mentality as a basis for observing all kinds of phenomena to see if they fitted in with this concept. I soon became convinced that it provided a clue to all kinds of things that had hitherto been obscure.

For instance, soon after I returned to Japan in 1956 it so happened that I saw two movies within a short span of time, one based on Murō Saisei's *Anzukko* and the other on Françoise Sagan's *Bonjour Tristesse*. Both portrayed the close relationship between father and daughter. In the former the father dotes on his daughter who returns home after an unfortunate marriage while in the latter there is a constant pull between the father and the daughter, each engaging in his or her own love affair. The home situations and the characters in the two stories are quite different, and it may be too hazardous to draw a conclusion from the comparison. Yet I could not help concluding that what is present in the closeness of the father-daughter relationship in Murō Saisei's story and missing in the other is the quality of *amaeru*, and that this, perhaps, is the chief characteristic of the Japanese parent-child relationship.

An episode that brought home still more strongly to me the uniqueness of the word *amae* as an item of vocabulary in Japanese occurred when I was asked to undertake treatment of a woman of mixed parentage who was suffering from anxiety hysteria. One day while I was questioning her mother concerning her upbringing the conversation turned to the patient's early childhood and the mother, an English lady born in Japan and fluent in Japanese, suddenly switched from English and said quite clearly in Japanese, *kono ko wa amari amaemasen deshita*—"She did not *amaeru* much" (in other words, she kept herself to herself, never "made up to" her parents, never behaved childishly in the confident assumption that her parents would indulge her). So admirably did this incident demonstrate both the uniqueness of the word *amae* and the universal significance of the phenomenon that it expresses that as soon as we came to a suitable pause in the conversation I asked her why she had used Japanese for that single sentence. She thought a while, then said, "There's no way of expressing it in English."

Quite apart from episodes such as this, which happen to illustrate the question very graphically, I became increasingly convinced, through everyday clinical observation, that the concept of *amae* was extremely useful in understanding the psychology of my patients. And in the same connection I began to realize that there were many other words, besides those I had dealt with in the paper I had given in America, that expressed states of mind related to *amae*—words such as *kigane* and *hinekureru*—and that they could all be used as aids in elucidating the abnormal psychology.

As a result, at the fifty-fourth conference of the Japan Psychiatric and Neurological Association in 1957, I presented my first research paper employing the *amae* concept and based on clinical experience.[5] In it, I made an analysis of the theory of *toraware* (preoccupation) in *shinkeishitsu* (nervousness), long knows as the "Morita theory," from the point of view of *amae*, and criticized it on the grounds that Morita was not correct in interpreting a neurotic patient's preoccupation with subjective symptoms as a result of excessive concentration of the attention. I next set out to show, via an analysis of observations made in treating patients, that the motive force behind this preoccupation was a frustrated desire to *amaeru*. This kind of analysis, I believed, would explain why the diagnosis of *shinkeishitsu* should have become so popular in Japan and why an exclusively Japanese theory of neurosis such as the "Morita theory" should have come into being. It also seemed to throw a light on the unique qualities of Japanese society. In short, I had the feeling in presenting this paper that I had struck an extremely rich vein of ore. I was intoxicated with the pregnant possibilities of the concept embodied in the word *amae*.

I subsequently developed these studies, seeking to examine all kinds of different pathologies of mind from the viewpoint of *amae*, and this led me in time to a realization of the close connection between *amae* and the awareness of the self as expressed in the Japanese word *jibun*. This word *jibun*, which is very rich in its implications, has concrete connotations quite different from the abstract feel of words such as *jiga* and *jiko* that are used to translate Western concepts of "self" or "ego". It is this that makes possible phrases such as *jibun ga aru* (he has a self), or *jibun ga nai* (he has no self).

In a paper[6] I read at the fifty-sixth conference of the Japanese Psychiatric and Neurological Association, I emphasized that this awareness of a *jibun* presumed the existence of an inner desire to *amaeru*, and made itself felt in opposition to that desire. To put it briefly, a man who has a *jibun* is capable of checking *amae*, while a man who is at the mercy of *amae* has no *jibun*. This is true of so-called normal people; persons with

19

schizophrenia, in whom the awareness of the self is abnormal, would seem to represent cases where there is a latent desire for *amae* but no experience of relations with others involving *amae*. From the outset, such persons have lacked the soil in which a proper sense of *jibun* could develop. It occurred to me that when such a person was placed in circumstances where he must check *amae*, he would be keenly aware of the lack of *jibun*.

One other question that was occupying my mind at the time when I delivered the two papers just outlined was how the psychology of *amae* related to general theories of psychological development. Since *amae* would seem to arise first as an emotion felt by the baby at the breast towards its mother, it must necessarily begin before establishment of the "Oedipus complex" of psychoanalytical theory. It corresponds to that tender emotion that, arising in earliest infancy, was labeled by Freud "the child's primary object-choice."[7]

It is obviously likely that it should have an influence on subsequent stages of development; Freud himself says so, yet for some reason or other he seems, particularly after his introduction of the concept of narcissism, to have attached comparatively little significance to it, and the views of the psychoanalysts who followed Freud are similar in this respect. It occurred to me that this might be because in the languages of the West there was no appropriate concept such as that of *amae*. One day in 1959 I happened to get hold of a copy of Michael Balint's *Primary Love and Psychoanalytic Technique*.[8] As I was reading it, I gradually realized with surprise and pleasure that what the author referred to by the forbidding name of "passive object love" was in fact none other than *amae*. My pleasure arose from a sense that my forecast that *amae* would prove to have an important significance psychoanalytically was backed up by Balint's studies. His remark, too, that "all the European languages fail to distinguish between active love and passive love" seemed to me to underline still more strongly my conviction

20

that the existence of an everyday word for passive love—*amae*—was an indicator of the nature of Japanese society and culture.

Eventually, the ideal chance came, in the form of an invitation to the tenth Pacific Science Congress held in Honolulu in the summer of 1961, to set in order and make public my findings concerning *amae*. For several years past I had been acquainted with William Caudill, an American social anthropologist who frequently visited Japan for research, and he had recommended me as a participant in a symposium on "Culture and Personality" at which he was to preside. The paper I presented was entitled "*Amae*—A Key Concept for Understanding Japanese Personality Structure."[9] In it, I summed up my findings so far on *amae*, pointing out that my conclusions tallied with the findings of American anthropologists such as Benedict and Candill, and that they also coincided with the conclusions of Nakamura Hajime—reached from a completely different scholarly viewpoint—concerning the ways of thinking of the Japanese.[10] Towards the end of my paper, I also dealt with the spiritual state of the Japanese since the end of the war, and argued that the postwar removal of the ideological restrictions imposed by the Emperor system and family system had not, at least directly, served the cause of individualism but by destroying the traditional channels of *amae* had contributed, if anything, to the spiritual and social confusion.

At the end of 1961, again at the recommendation of William Candill, I was invited as visiting scientist to the National Institute of Mental Health at Bethesda in Maryland. During the total of fourteen months I spent there, I had a fresh opportunity to see how American psychiatrists dealt with their patients in practice. I frequently observed interviews with patients and their relatives conducted in rooms with one-way mirrors. I began to feel that, generally speaking, American psychiatrists were extraordinarily insensitive to the feelings of helplessness of their patients. In other words, they were slow to

detect the concealed *amae* of their patients. This merely recon-
firmed, this time via psychiatric patients, what I myself had
experienced when I first came to America.

I subsequently asked a considerable number of psychiatrists
for their views on how one should deal with various hypothetical
situations in interviewing patients, and their replies only led
me to the same conclusion. Although I foresaw this to a certain
extent, I was still rather surprised to find that even psychiatrists,
who laid claim to being specialists on the psyche and the
emotions—and those, moreover, who had received a psychoanalytical training—should be so slow to detect the *amae*, the
need for a passive love, that lay in the deepest parts of the
patient's mind. It brought home to me anew the inevitability
of cultural conditioning.

While I was in America I wrote a paper entitled "Some
Thoughts on Helplessness," based on these observations. It was
originally written for lectures that I gave when I was invited
to the departments of psychiatry at Pittsburgh and Yale universities and the Washington School of Psychiatry, but it was
later published in a psychiatric journal under the title "Some
Thoughts on Helplessness and the Desire to be Loved."[11] In
this paper, I discussed the differences in cultural backgrounds
between East and West and argued that the criterion of self-
reliance that was assumed in psychoanalysis and psychiatry
was admirable and undoubtedly indispensable as a goal to be
achieved by the patient, but that when it became, not simply
a guiding principle in the course of the treatment, but something to which the doctor conformed unthinkingly, it tended in
effect to abandon the patient to his helplessness and even make
it impossible to understand the patient's true state of mind.

What I was doing, in fact, was to make some observations of
the state of psychiatry in America from the viewpoint of *amae*.
At the same time, I was casting a critical glance at the whole
of Western civilization that lay in the background. As one proof

of the prominence of the spirit of self-reliance in the modern Western world, I pointed out the popularity since the seventeenth century of the saying "The Lord helps those who help themselves." I also discussed Freud's theories of religion,[12] according to which the danger in religion is that it uses faith in God as an easy way of appeasing man's sense of impotence, and argued that it was, rather, the anthropocentrism in which Freud himself put his faith that was being used in practice to remove that sense of impotence. To me this seemed to be borne out by the indifference towards the patient's sense of helplessness shown by most American psychiatrists influenced by psychoanalytic theory.

During my stay in America I was invited to a conference on the modernization of Japan held in Bermuda in January 1963 under the chairmanship of Professor Ronald Dore. My paper entitled "*Giri Ninjō*—an Interpretation"[13] was an amplification and development of "*Amae*—a Key Concept for Understanding the Japanese Personality Structure" that I had read in Honolulu in 1961. In it, I pointed out that the *amae* psychology lay at the core of the concepts of *giri* and *ninjō* (to be discussed later) that had fashioned the moral outlook of the Japanese since long before the Meiji Restoration. I also argued that the Emperor system established by the Meiji government, insofar as it set up a spiritual focus for the state transcending class and social strata, represented an attempt at modernization based on the traditional ideas of *giri* and *ninjō*. I further discussed the spiritual confusion of the period following Japan's defeat in World War II, referring in the course of my argument to the marked sense of being victimized in the Japanese pointed out by Maruyama Masao in his *Nihon no Shisō*,[14] and suggested a close connection between this sense and the psychology of *amae*. This question of the sense of grievance went on fermenting in my mind thereafter; in particular, I find it of absorbing importance in its relation to the social situation in recent years, and for this reason I shall be discussing it again later.

Shortly after the Bermuda conference I returned to Japan. The first thing I did following my return was a revision of *Psychoanalysis*[15] which I had published (in Japanese) in 1956, and I decided that this was an opportunity for a fundamental reconsideration of the theories of psychoanalysis in the light of my findings concerning *amae*. The idea had been in my mind ever since I read Balint's essay, and I had published a few papers on the subject myself, but I now tackled the question on a broad front.

My work bore fruit in 1965 in a book with the revised title of *Psychoanalysis and Psychopathology*.[16] As I wrote in my preface, the concept of *amae* had become for me a central concept in understanding psychoanalytical theory, so much so that I found it odd that Freud could have built his theory without it. Admittedly, Freud is not without other concepts to take its place. As I have said, relatively little significance was attributed in Freud's theories to the infantile desire for love, but this is because it is discussed, under a different guise, as homosexual feeling, Freud's theory being that it plays a pathological role in neurosis and psychosis. I first made public my ideas on this subject at a conference on "Neurosis and Japanese Characteristics" in the autumn of 1963.[17] It seemed to me, indeed, that the fact that in the West the feelings experienced in Japan as *amae* would normally only be interpreted as homosexual feelings was an admirable reflection of the cultural and social discrepancies between the two sides (for further discussion of this point, see the section on "Homosexual Feelings" in chapter four).

My reconsideration of the theories of psychoanalysis from the viewpoint of *amae* and my simultaneous observation from the same viewpoint of the characteristics of the Japanese gradually persuaded me to look at the problems of modern society from the same angle. In 1960, I wrote a short piece entitled "Momotarō and Zengakuren"[18] in which I set out, in my own fashion, to consider the significance of the Zengakuren* student movement that was beginning to create such a stir around that time. My reason for likening the students to Momotarō** was their enthusiasm for quelling demons in the manner of Momotarō and because it seemed to me that the manner of Momotarō's birth—not from parents, but from a peach—symbolically suggested the generation gap so evident in the students participating in the movement.

I developed the same theme in more detail in 1968 in a short contribution to a newspaper entitled "The Psychology of Today's Rebellious Youth"[19] (reproduced here in the section on "The Rebellion of Youth" in chapter five). This piece was inspired by the student movement which happened to have flared up again around that time, but in both articles I refused to dismiss the students, as some commentators did, simply as "presuming on society's indulgence" (*amaeru*). It was not that in my view they were not "presuming"; they were "presuming" without doubt, but it seemed to me that the situation that had developed was too complex to discuss it solely in these terms. As I saw it, still more serious than their *amae* was the decline of society's authority.

Subsequently, as the student movement became still more violent, and with the growing hold on young people gained by the theories of violence peculiar to the New Left movement known as Zenkyōtō,*** I had an increasingly hard time trying to

---

* The National Federation of Students' Self-Governing Bodies, a radical student organization first formed in 1948 and noted for its violently left-wing activities, which reached a peak during the 1950's and early 1960's.
** The hero of one of the most celebrated Japanese children's tales. Born from a peach, he was brought up by the old man and woman who found him, and on growing up proved himself by setting off, accompanied only by a dog, a monkey, and a pheasant, to quell the demons on Demons' Island.
*** "Joint Struggle Committees," another of the student left-wing organizations that proliferated in the 1950's and 1960's but have since been undermined by increasing factionalism and public opposition to their methods.

interpret the phenomenon for myself. The thing that most interested me was the odd way in which the students of Zenkyō-tō, though behaving as victimizers, frequently aroused in their victims a sense that they themselves were the victimizers. Thinking about this, I came to the conclusion that the reason was, ultimately, that the students were putting themselves in the position of victims. I wrote a magazine article entitled "The Sense of Guilt and the Sense of Grievance,"[20] and the sense of grievance that I had noted earlier in writing about *giri* and *ninjō* began to look extremely significant indeed to me.

The man with a sense of grievance does not simply nourish an individual sense of being a victim but identifies with victims in general—oppressed peoples, the poor, the mentally sick and so on. In that they cannot *amaeru* they are beyond doubt victims, yet at the same time they can be said to be taking advantage of (*amaete iru*) their position as victims. I realized, too, that this psychology was a factor common to the rebellion of youth affecting the whole world. Moreover, I found it rather surprising and also highly suggestive that the convenient and popular term *higaisha-ishiki* (sense of grievance, sense of being victimized) should be an item of vocabulary especially familiar to Japanese. The emotional youth of today probably derive their feeling of grievance from an awareness of the threat looming over the whole world, in which sense the feeling of victimization might well be called the spirit of the modern age.

In the chapters that follow I shall develop in detail the findings on *amae* of which I have outlined the history above. In "The World of *Amae*," I shall try to show that *amae* is a thread that runs through all the various activities of Japanese society. Next, in the chapter entitled "The Logic of *Amae*," I shall examine the psychological structure implied by the term *amae*, and discuss its relationship to the spiritual culture of Japan. In "The Pathology of *Amae*," I give an account, as far as is possible without going into specialist discussions, of the abnormal forms into which *amae* is sometimes transformed. Then finally, in "*Amae* and Modern Society," I shall discuss various problems of modern society from the viewpoint of *amae*.

2 The world of *amae*

The fact that, as we have already seen in the preceding chapter, the word *amae* is, as a word, peculiar to the Japanese language yet describes a psychological phenomenon that is basically common to mankind as a whole shows not only how especially familiar the psychology in question is to the Japanese but also that the Japanese social structure is formed in such a way as to permit expression of that psychology. This implies in turn that *amae* is a key concept for the understanding not only of the psychological makeup of the individual Japanese but of the structure of Japanese society as a whole. The emphasis on vertical relationships that social anthropologist Nakane Chie[21] recently stipulated as characteristic of the Japanese-type social structure could also be seen as an emphasis on *amae*. One might be justified, even, in seeing the susceptibility to *amae* as the cause of this emphasis on vertical relationships. In the following pages I hope to show, by examining a number of terms that have a definitive influence on the Japanese outlook, just how deeply Japanese society is permeated by the concept of *amae*.

The vocabulary of *amae*

The word *amae* itself is far from being an isolated expression of the *amae* psychology in the Japanese language. A large number of other words give expression to the same psychology.

The adjective *amai*, for example, is used not only in the sense of "sweet" to the taste, but also as a description of a man's character: thus if A is said to be *amai* to B, it means that he allows B to *amaeru*, i.e. to behave self-indulgently, presuming on some special relationship that exists between the two. It is also said that a person's view of a situation is *amai*, which means that it is excessively optimistic, without a proper grasp of the realities at stake, the cause of this misapprehension, presumably, being that the person concerned is allowing wishful thinking (a form of self-indulgence) to get the better of his judgment. In the same way the word *amanzuru*, defined by the dictionaries as to be satisfied with something, to put up with it because there is no better alternative, could surely be interpreted as someone's allowing himself to feel that he is being self-indulgent when in fact the situation does not really call for it. The best thing, in short, is to be able to indulge the desire for *amae*, but when that is not possible one makes do with *amanzuru*.

Next, there is a group of words such as *suneru, higamu, hinekureru,* and *uramu* that relate to various states of mind brought about by the inability to *amaeru*. *Suneru* (to be sulky) occurs when one is not allowed to be straightforwardly self-indulgent, yet the attitude comprises in itself a certain degree of that same self-indulgence. *Futekusareru* and *yakekuso ni naru* (indicating, respectively, the attitudes of defiance and irresponsibility in speech or behavior associated with a "fit of the sulks,") are two phenomena that arise as a result of *suneru*. *Higamu* (to be suspicious or jaundiced in one's attitude), which involves laboring under the delusion that one is being treated unjustly, has its origins in the failure of one's desire for indulgence to find the expected response. *Hinekureru* (to behave in a distorted, perverse way) involves feigning indifference to the other instead of showing *amae*. Under the surface one is, in fact, concerned with the other's reaction; although there appears to be no *amae*, it is there, basically, all the time. *Uramu* (to show resent-

29

ment toward or hatred of) means that rejection of one's *amae* has aroused feelings of hostility; this hostility has a complexity, not present in simple hatred, that shows how closely it is linked with the *amae* psychology. I recall how, during the meeting mentioned earlier with M. Balint in 1964, he was fascinated to hear that in Japanese there was not only an everyday word corresponding to his "passive object love" but a word—*uramu*—expressing the special type of hostility arising from its frustration.

Next, we must examine words such as *tanomu*, *toriiru*, *kodawaru*, *kigane*, *wadakamari*, and *tereru*. The word *tanomu* is discussed by R. P. Dore in his *City Life in Japan*,[22] in which he singles it out for mention as a word with a sense roughly midway between the English "to ask" and "to rely on," implying that one is entrusting some matter concerning oneself personally to another person in the expectation that he will handle it in a manner favorable to oneself. Dore's interpretation is completely correct. *Tanomu*, in other words, means nothing other than "I hope you will permit my self-indulgence." Next, *toriiru* means to curry favor with the other man as a means of achieving one's own ends; it is a method of permitting oneself to *amaeru* while appearing to allow it to the other man. A man, now, who "*kodawaru*'s," or makes difficulties, is one who in his relationships with others is not easily given to "asking" or "being made up to." Even more than the average man, of course, he would like to be permitted self-indulgence, but the fear of being rejected prevents him from giving it straightforward expression. *Kigane* and *wadakamari* represent very similar states of mind. *Kigane* (restraint) implies a constant feeling of *enryo* (consideration) towards the other person as a result of apprehension lest he fail to accept one's own *amae* as unreservedly as one might wish. *Wadakamari* is used when an ostensible indifference conceals a lurking resentment towards the other man. The man who looks embarrassed or awkward (*tereru*), too, resembles the man who creates difficulties (*kodawaru*) in his inability to give his own desire for indulgence straightforward expression, but his trouble is not fear of rejection so much as shame at revealing his self-indulgence before others.

Next, I should like to discuss the concept of *sumanai* in some detail, since the term is rather special in that it is used to express both gratitude and apology, two seemingly very different situations. In *The Chrysanthemum and the Sword*, Ruth Benedict devotes a considerable number of pages to discussion of this word, which shows that its precise shade of meaning occupied her greatly. I myself see *sumanai* as the regular negative form of the verb *sumu*, meaning to end or be completed as used of some action or task. This differs from the view of the late Yanagida Kunio,[23] who saw it as the negative of the verb *sumu* meaning to be clear or free from impurities, but I cannot help feeling that my interpretation is more consistent with the way the word is used in practice. In other words, the matter is "not ended"—something is still left over—because one has not done everything one should have done. Thus it expresses a strong feeling of apology towards the other person—and it is precisely for this reason that the word *sumanai* is also used to thank him for his kindness. One uses it, in other words, in the assumption that the kind deed has been a burden to the doer, and not, as Ruth Benedict suggests, from any immediate consciousness of the need to *repay* the kindness.

Benedict is doubtless right, of course, in pointing out that the Japanese tend to show the same psychological approach to two such differing circumstances as helping each other and monetary exchanges. The question here, however, is why the Japanese are not content simply to show gratitude for a kind action but must apologize for the trouble which they imagine it has caused the other person. The reason is that they fear that unless they apologize the other man will think them impolite with the result that they may lose his good will. And this, it seems,

31

accounts for the frequency of the word *sumanai*—the desire not to lose the other's good will, to be permitted the same degree of self-indulgence indefinitely. I shall return later to the psychology underlying the use of *sumanai* just discussed, since it is related to the Japanese sense of guilt and shame, and also to the question of why the Western concept of freedom is slow to take root in Japan.

In addition to the words already discussed there are phrases which use verbs meaning, literally, eat (*kuu*), drink (*nomu*), and lick (*nameru*) to express various assumed attitudes of superiority or contempt in dealing with the other person, and which might seem at first sight to have no relationship with *amae*. Japanese is not, of course, the only language that uses verbs originally connected with food in reference to human relationships, but what is interesting in the case of Japanese is that they all imply a lack of *amae*. The man who "eats," "drinks," or "licks" others seems active and confident on the surface, but inside he is alone and helpless. He has not really transcended *amae*; rather, he behaves as he does in order to cover up a lack of *amae*. For example, a speaker who "swallows" his audience is a man who would otherwise tend to be "swallowed" by it instead, and assumes an overbearing attitude in order to avoid this happening. It is the same with "eating" people, (in the case of "eat or be eaten" in particular, the struggle becomes a matter of life or death). Again, the rough's threatening "think you can lick (*nameru*) me, do you?" or the use of the same expression in relations between the sexes indicates a lack of true human contact based on mutual recognition of each other's need for indulgence. In this sense, one might see *amae* as an essential factor smoothing the path of human exchanges in Japan.

Giri and *ninjō*

A great deal has been written by scholars, both Japanese and foreign alike, on the theme of *giri* and *ninjō*—roughly translatable as social obligation and human feeling—but a work recently published by Minamoto Ryōen, "*Giri* and *Ninjō*—A Study of the Japanese Mentality,"[24] besides making a study of material that has appeared on the subject so far, is especially interesting for its ambitious attempt to survey the twin theme as it is reflected in literature. My aim here is to bypass such examination of documentary evidence and make two observations concerning the question from a purely psychological point of view. The first is that *ninjō* and *giri* indicate responses that have a close bearing on *amae*. The second is that *ninjō* and *giri* are not simply opposed but would seem to exist in a kind of organic relationship to each other. It is clear from the frequent remark made by Japanese that "foreigners do not understand *ninjō*," or, conversely, that "even foreigners have *ninjō* too" that *ninjō* does not refer simply to human feeling as a whole. In short, they seem to be unconsciously aware that what seems to be a general appellation has come in practice to refer to a set of emotions that are especially familiar to the Japanese themselves —which is probably only to be expected when one considers that, as we have seen, all the many Japanese words dealing with human relations reflect some aspect of the *amae* mentality. This does not mean, of course, that the average man is clearly aware of *amae* as the central emotion in *ninjō*. Nevertheless, it seems almost certain that the things understood as *ninjō* are apprehended vaguely as a kind of *Gestalt*, and that it is the ability or failure of foreigners to fall in with this that gives rise to remarks about foreigners understanding or not understanding *ninjō*.

Next, there is the question of the nature of *giri*. This seems to be definable as the feeling involved in the type of relationship that, unlike relationships such as those between parent and child or between siblings, in which *ninjō* occurs spontaneously, have *ninjō* brought into them, as it were, artificially. This means that *giri* relationships, whether with relatives, between master and pupil, between friends, or even with neighbors, are all in areas where it is officially permitted to experience *ninjō*. If this idea, which Sato Tadao has expressed in the phrase "*giri* continually aspires toward *ninjō*"[25] is correct, then one must conclude that Benedict and others were wrong in considering the *ninjō* circle and the *giri* circle as essentially in opposition to each other, since it is possible to consider *giri* as the vessel, as it were, and *ninjō* as the content. Even the parent-child relationship may be experienced as *giri* when the relationship itself is stressed at the expense of the natural affection. For example, while the famous saying by Shigemori, "If I wish to be loyal to the Emperor, I can't be filial to my father" is usually taken as indicating the clash of *giri* and *ninjō*, it would be more correct to interpret it as indicating a conflict occurring between two different *giri*. Nor is this the only case; all situations, in fact, where the subject seems at first sight to be trapped between the claims of *giri* and *ninjō* are, strictly speaking, a clash between *giri* and *giri*, in other words a conflict that is implicit in *ninjō* as such.

In order to make this point still clearer, let us consider the relationship between the concept of *on* and *giri*. There is a saying in Japanese "to incur *on* through a single night's stay." As this suggests, *on* implies the receiving of some kindness—i.e. *ninjō*—from another, and also implies that *on* calls into existence a *giri*. To put it differently, *on* means that one has incurred a kind of psychological burden as a result of receiving a favor, while *giri* means that *on* has brought about a relationship of interdependence. Now, what is usually referred to as the clash of *giri* and *ninjō* can surely be seen as a case where there is an opposition between a number of persons from whom one has received *on*, so that to fulfil one's *giri* towards one of them will mean neglecting it toward another. For the person concerned, of course, the ideal thing would be to keep the good will of all concerned, and it is the difficulty or impossibility of doing so that causes the conflict. The essence of the conflict, in other words, is not so much that one has to retain one and reject the other, but that one is forced to make the choice against one's own will. In other words, the motive force behind the inner conflict is the desire to retain good will: which means, of course, one's *amae*. An interesting fact in this connection is that the emotion expressed in the word *sumanai* is experienced most often in *giri* relationships. Japanese do, in fact, exchange the word *sumanai* very frequently in this situation, and this is perfectly natural when one considers, as has already been explained, that the word *sumanai* is used as a means of holding on to the other's good will.

It will be clear from the preceding that both *giri* and *ninjō* have their roots deep in *amae*. To put it briefly, to emphasize *ninjō* is to affirm *amae*, to encourage the other person's sensitivity towards *amae*. To emphasize *giri*, on the other hand, is to stress the human relationships contracted via *amae*. Or one might replace *amae* by the more abstract term "dependence," and say that *ninjō* welcomes dependence whereas *giri* binds human beings in a dependent relationship. The Japanese society of the past, in which *giri* and *ninjō* were the predominant ethical concepts, might without exaggeration be described as a world pervaded throughout by *amae*.

Tanin and *enryo*

The Japanese word *tanin* is an odd expression. Literally, the two Chinese characters with which it is written mean "other people," but in practice another word, *tasha*, (also meaning, literally, others) has had to be invented where it is necessary to indicate people other than oneself in the strict sense. If one looks up *tanin* in a Japanese dictionary, the first definition given is "persons with no blood relationship to oneself," while the second is "persons unconnected with oneself." Thus the essential meaning lies in the absence of blood relationship, and it is the parent-child relationship that obviously lies farthest from *tanin*.

On the other hand ties such as those of man and wife, or those acquired via the parental relationship, such as those of brothers and sisters, have a potential *tanin* quality; it is said that "husband and wife were once basically *tanin*" and that "*tanin* begin with one's brothers." Parents and children, however, cannot become *tanin*, since the ties binding them are considered to be unbreakable; and indeed there would seem to be a tendency in Japan to look on this parent-child relationship as the ideal and to use it as a yardstick in judging all other relationships. A relationship between two people becomes deeper the closer it approaches to the warmth of the parent-child relationship, and is considered shallow unless it becomes so. In other words, no relationship between people is a real relationship so long as they remain *tanin*. It is for this reason that *tanin* means someone who has no connection with oneself. The word *tanin* does, in fact, have for the Japanese a ring of coldness and indifference, as is perfectly clear if one considers expressions such as "a complete *tanin*," "*tanin* don't care," "*tanin* matters" (i.e. which are no concern of one's own).

To digress a little, the title of Camus' novel *L'Etranger*, which is usually rendered in Japanese as *Ihōjin* (meaning "a person from another land," "a foreigner"), would surely be more correctly rendered as *tanin*, as in the English, *The Outsider*. The chief character, hearing that his mother, from whom he has long been separated, has died at the old folks' home where she has been living, goes to attend her funeral, but feels no emotion whatsoever. Shortly afterwards, he embarks on a relationship with a woman, and also becomes involved by chance in a dispute as a result of which he ends up killing a man. However, since he has not been driven to the murder by any violent emotion, he fails correspondingly to feel any remorse at his trial. He has become alienated from his mother, from his acquaintances, from all men. All other people have become *tanin*—or perhaps he has become a *tanin* for them. What is interesting here is that whereas in French the word *étranger* is used to express his situation, in Japanese the word *tanin* is quite adequate. To translate *étranger* here as *ihōjin* (one from another country; foreigner) is particularly inappropriate in Japan, I feel, where foreigners tend to be objects of curiosity rather than indifference. It is true, admittedly, that the same word *ihōjin* has long been used in the Japanese version of the Bible as a translation of the contemptuous Jewish term "gentile," and that it comes closer to the meaning of *tanin* if taken in this sense.

Now, the fact that the parent-child relationship is the only one that is unrestrictedly *not* a *tanin* relationship, while other relationships become increasingly *tanin* as they move farther away from this basic relationship is interesting in that this also coincides with the use of the word *amaeru*. In other words, it is the most natural thing in the world for *amae* to exist in the parent-child relationship, while other cases where *amae* comes into play would all seem to be either quasi-parental relationships or relationships in which there is some element of this basic relationship. One might express it diagrammatically, using the concepts of *giri* and *ninjō*, in the following fashion. The parent-child relationship where *amae* arises naturally is the world of *ninjō* (spontaneously arising feeling); relationships where it is permitted to introduce *amae* form the world of *giri* (socially contracted interdependence); the unrelated world unaffected by either *ninjō* or *giri* is inhabited by *tanin*, "others." As I just said, this is diagrammatic: the three worlds just described are not, of course, so clearly defined in reality, nor, as we have seen, are *ninjō* and *giri* in the strictest sense opposed, but stand in the relationship of content and vessel; thus the parent-child relationship that ought properly speaking to be rich in *ninjō* may become cold *giri*, while a *giri* relationship may abound in *ninjō*. Again, while *tanin* are unrelated to oneself so long as they remain *tanin*, it should not be forgotten that *giri* binds together those who were originally *tanin*; in this sense, even *tanin* have a constant potential for entering on relationships of *amae*.

At this point let us glance at the term *enryo*, another peculiarly Japanese expression which may be translated roughly as "restraint" or "holding back." This word was originally used, apparently, to mean thoughtful consideration in the literal sense of the two characters with which it is written—*en*, distant, *ryo*, consideration—but nowadays it is chiefly used as a negative yardstick in measuring the intimacy of human relationships. In the parent-child relationship there is no *enryo*, since parents and their children are not *tanin*, the relationship being permeated with *amae*. In this case, not only does the child feel no *enryo* toward the parent, but the parent equally feels no *enryo* toward the child. With other relationships outside this parent-child relationship, *enryo* decreases proportionately with intimacy and increases with distance. There are relationships, such as those between friends, in which there is a great absence of *enryo*; indeed, the Japanese expression *shinyū* ("close friend") indicates precisely this type of relationship. In their hearts, in

38

other words, the Japanese do not care much for *enryo*. Everybody believes that if possible an absence of *enryo* is ideal, which is itself a reflection of the fact that, basically, the Japanese idealize the kind of relationship of oneness typically embodied in the parent-child relationship.

Enryo has almost the same meaning as the words *kigane* and *kodawari* which I have discussed previously. In other words, one holds back with the idea that one must not presume too much (*amaeru*) on the other's good will. The fear is at work, in other words, that unless one holds back, one will be thought impertinent and disliked accordingly. One might say that *enryo* is an inverted form of *amae*.

Generally speaking, then, *enryo* is felt to be a confining state of mind and disliked as such, but there are also times when people realize its value. While one may remark, for example, "I have some feeling of *enryo* that makes it difficult to talk to him," in which case the *enryo* is undesirable, there are also remarks implying that it would be desirable, such as "He really ought to show more *enryo*." Furthermore, it frequently happens that discord between parents and children, or the estrangement of close friends, is attributed to a lack of *enryo* between the parties concerned.

The Japanese, generally speaking, tend to dislike *enryo* in themselves but to expect it in others, a fact which is probably accounted for by the way in which the *amae* mentality dominates social life. Here also would seem to lie the reason why the idea of privacy—which more than anything else, perhaps, sets store by "considering from a distance"—did not traditionally develop in Japan. This question will naturally crop up again in the next section on "inside" and "outside."

Inside and outside

The presence or absence of *enryo* is used by the Japanese as a gauge in distinguishing between the types of human relationship that they refer to as "outer" and "inner." One's relatives, with whom no *enryo* is necessary, are in one's "inner" circle—literally, since the term *miuchi*, "relatives," means something like "one's inner circle"—but *giri*-type relationships where *enryo* is present are the "outer" circle. Sometimes, however, *giri* relationships and acquaintanceships are themselves regarded as "inner" in contrast to the world of *tanin* with whom one is quite unconnected, and where there is no need, even, to bring *enryo* into play. In either case, the gauge for distinguishing between inner and outer is the presence or absence of *enryo*. This distinction is one that any Japanese makes, yet even so it is not believed to be a good thing that the difference between an individual's attitude to inner and outer should be too extreme. To say of someone, for instance, that "he's good outside but bad inside" is a rather disapproving expression signifying that the person in question is selfish and difficult in dealing with family members yet in his "outer" relationships passes for a pleasant and considerate man. Similar is the case of the *uchi-Benkei* ("indoor Benkei," an allusion to a hero of popular legend), who lords it in his own home but is weak as soon as he steps outside. A different type again is the man who is pleasant in personal contacts yet behaves with complete indifference towards outsiders who have no connection with him. So, too, it is with the type of man—familiar from the proverb "the traveler discards his sense of shame"—who is diffident and circumspect in the place where he lives, yet in strange surroundings behaves just as the fancy takes him. The Japanese as a whole are often criticized for this trait by people of other countries.

Thus although a distinction exists between "inner" and "outer," the implication is different depending on whether human relations in which a certain degree of *enryo* is at work are considered as inside or outside. If one takes relationships in which *enryo* is at work as a kind of middle zone, one has on the inner side of it members of one's family with whom there is no *enryo*, and on the outer side strangers (*tanin*) with whom the need for *enryo* does not occur. What is interesting is that although the innermost world and the outermost world seem to be cut off from each other, they also have, insofar as the individual's attitude towards them is without *enryo*, something in common. In the case of relatives, however, the absence of *enryo* is due to *amae*, whereas the same cannot be said of the absence of *enryo* towards "strangers." In the former case, there is no holding back because the relationship of *amae* means there are no barriers, whereas in the latter case barriers exist but there is no holding back since the barriers are not consciously felt. It is significant that both a high degree of *amae* and its total absence should give rise to the same lack of concern for others. Indeed, one often finds that it is precisely the man showing the most self-indulgent *amae* toward his family who shows the greatest coldness and indifference toward strangers. This, it would seem, is the same kind of approach to relationships with others that I referred to in discussing terms such as *kuu*, *nomu*, and *nameru* in the section on "The Vocabulary of *Amae*"; in brief, the man who is normally accustomed to *amae* behaves in a superior or contemptuous way when he finds himself in a position where he cannot *amaeru*.

Now, since most Japanese consider it perfectly natural that a man should vary his attitude depending on whether he is dealing with his "inner circle" or with others, no one considers it hypocritical or contradictory that he should behave wilfully within his own circle yet control himself outside it. Nor are they particularly shocked should a man who normally shows great self-control kick over the traces in a place where he is not known. That a man's standards of behavior should differ within his own circle and outside it affords no food for inner conflict. This only holds true, however, so long as the outer dividing line is clearly defined; should it become vague, trouble occurs. A good example is the "If I wish to be loyal to the Emperor, I can't be filial to my father," which I quoted in the section on "*Giri* and *Ninjō.*" The trouble here is that a conflict has arisen between the object of loyalty and the object of filial devotion, so that it has become impossible to maintain the distinctions hitherto observed between the two. The uncomfortable thing is not any inner conflict arising from differing standards of attitude and action, but being forced to make a choice and being unable to presume on *amae* any longer. It is surely significant in this connection that the Japanese term *uchi* (inside) as used in words such as *miuchi* (family circle) or *nakamauchi* (circle of friends or colleagues) refers mainly to the group to which the individual belongs and not, as with English terms such as "private," to the individual himself. In Japan, little value is attributed to the individual's private realm as distinct from the group. This is related to the fact, which I have already pointed out, that ideas of privacy which would attribute a positive value to *enryo* have always been wanting in Japan. It also has a bearing on the fact—which I shall return to later—that the Western idea of freedom has been slow to take root in Japan.

Not only has Japan failed to establish the freedom of the individual as distinct from the group, but there is, it seems, a serious dearth of the type of public spirit that transcends both individual and group. This, too, would seem to have its origins in the fact that the Japanese divide their lives into inner and outer sectors each with its own, different, standards of behavior, no one feeling the slightest oddity in this discrepancy. The Japanese behave "reasonably" when *enryo* is present, but the circle in which *enryo* must be exerted is itself experienced as an "inner" circle in relation to the outside world where no *enryo* is necessary, and is not "public" in the true sense of the word. The distinction between "inner" and "outer" is relevant, mostly, to the individual. It is socially approved, moreover, which is why the public spirit does not develop.

Where the distinction between inner and outer is clear, but not that between private and public, it is no wonder that the private and the public should be confused or that public property should be put to private use. The same reason probably accounts for the way factions—whether based on school, clan, intermarriage, financial interest, or military affiliation—have always been prone to take charge and become political forces. Of course, the rule of the faction is hardly an exclusively Japanese phenomenon. In the same way, the distinction between inner and outer circles, so marked in Japan, is not a uniquely Japanese invention but is common to all mankind. Nevertheless, it is still safe to say that in Western society at least there has always been, on the one hand, a spirit of individual freedom transcending the group and, on the other, a public spirit.

A function corresponding roughly to the public spirit has traditionally been fulfilled in Japan by the idea of *ōyake* or *honke*. The term *ōyake*, often translatable as "public" or "the public sector" originally referred to the Imperial family; so both *ōyake* and *honke* (the main branch of a family) in themselves represent the most time-hallowed cliques of all, and cannot for this reason represent the "public" in the true sense. In fact, it often happened that other factions vied with each other in the attempt to draw *ōyake*, as the primary faction, to their own side. Yet one might still say that *ōyake* has prevented

43

any other faction from expanding its power into a dictatorship, and has even to some extent served to check struggles among other factions. This is why, it seems, the word *ōyake* was selected when it became necessary to translate the word "public" into Japanese. Particularly since the end of the war and the clear separation of the word *ōyake* from the sense of "Imperial family," there has been a great deal of talk about the "public spirit" in the Western sense. Even so, it is undeniable that the old "*ōyake* spirit" still pervades the Japanese mentality. The Imperial family may have retired into the background; but government still centers round the faction, and the strongest faction still represents *ōyake*.

Nor is this phenomenon confined to the establishment, being equally apparent among anti-establishment movements. A good example is to be seen in the inter-factional strife seen in extreme-leftist student movements in recent years. The same tendency is not restricted to the political sphere; the factional outlook makes itself felt in every aspect of the spiritual life of the Japanese, with the result that wherever one goes one comes across "petty emperors." The reason would seem to be that the criterion for Japanese behavior is the distinction between the inner circle and outer circle, with no firmly established individual freedom or public spirit.

Identification and assimilation

We have seen that the apportioning of life into inner and outer sections by the Japanese takes the form, strictly speaking, of three concentric circles, the strangers in the outermost circle being treated with indifference or lack of *enryo*. This only applies, however, when the stranger presents no threat; once the threat occurs, the attitude changes abruptly. It is possible to see this attitude as an exaggerated reaction due to the fact that

44

even at times of apparent coldness and indifference a latent threat is, in fact, felt. One could say, in other words, that the tendency to show an attitude of lofty superiority or indifference is an attempt, by means of such a pose, to intimidate the other side before one is intimidated oneself. If these means—indifference or intimidation—do not succeed, resort must be made to some other means. And the means used at this point is to win favor with (*toriiru*) or take over (*torikomu*) the other side. This process corresponds with what is known in psychoanalysis as identification or assimilation, but it is significant here that we have already encountered the word *toriiru* in the section on "The Vocabulary of *Amae*." *Torikomu*, again, can be seen as a kind of "spiritual ingestion." As this suggests very clearly, identification and assimilation are psychological mechanisms with which the inhabitants of the world of *amae* are very much at home.

The preceding applies, of course, to individuals, but interestingly enough it can also be applied to Japan as a whole. This is particularly true of the times in the past when Japan first came into contact with foreign cultures, when its reaction can be explained largely in terms of identification and assimilation. In this connection, the following quotation from the work of Nakamura Hajime is very illuminating: "Generally speaking, in adopting foreign religions, the Japanese have already had some practical ethical framework which they regard as absolute, and have taken over and adapted only insofar as the newcomer would not damage, or would actually encourage and develop, what already existed. No doubt, those who fervently embraced the new religions were sincerely pious in their individual hearts, but even so Japanese society as a whole did no more than take over for its own purposes."[26] In the language of *amae*, "take over for its own purposes" as Nakamura uses it signifies *toriiru* and *torikomu*. And the "practical, ethical framework which they regard as absolute" that he cites as the single

45

condition for taking over can be seen as the stress on *amae* in human relationships. To express what Nakamura says in rather different terms, one might say that although the Japanese seem at first glance to accept foreign culture uncritically, at the same time, paradoxically enough, the attitude that accepts and adopts everything that can be accepted and adopted uncritically helps to preserve the *amae* psychology, since the action of accepting and adopting is, in itself, an extension of that mentality.

In fact, the Japanese showed the same pattern in the way they took over the culture of China, the culture of the Portugese, and, in more recent times, the culture of the West as a whole. One has only to read an essay by Lafcadio Hearn entitled "A Glance at the Trends."[27] to see vividly the process whereby the Japanese of early Meiji times at first skillfully "made up to" Western culture as embodied in the foreign settlements—or, more accurately, in the bearers of foreign culture—then finally "devoured" them voraciously. The national policy of modern Japan, beginning with the Sino-Japanese and Russo-Japanese wars and continuing right through to the Greater East Asia War, was permeated by the determination to join the ranks of the Western powers by imitation and adoption of things Western. The industrialization that has been carried out at such a frantic pace since Japan's defeat in the last war can be seen, similarly, as inspired by the same national motives.

I have referred here to historical and social facts because they are excellent examples of the Japanese attitude to the outside world. As I have already pointed out, the Japanese tend to ignore the world of strangers, but even this is far from meaning a lack of interest. They ignore the outside world in so far as they judge this to be possible, but even when they appear to be indifferent they are in fact keeping a formidably watchful eye on their surroundings. And once they have realized that something cannot be ignored, they busily set about identifying with and adopting it.

In this connection, I should say something here concerning the much commented-on curiosity of the Japanese. This curiosity was noticed long ago by foreigners visiting this country. As early as the sixteenth century, Francisco Xavier, the first Christian missionary to arrive in Japan, remarked in his letters on the extraordinary desire for knowledge of the Japanese, in which respect they were, he said admiringly, different from any other heathens.[28] This curiosity and lust for knowledge was certainly an important contribution to the fact that Japan modernized herself at an earlier date than any other Oriental nation. The Chinese afford a strong contrast with the Japanese in this respect. The Chinese have for the most part regarded Western civilization with contempt, as the following excerpt from the autobiography of Lu Hsün shows: "The orthodox course at that time was to study the Confucian classics and take the government service examination; those who studied Western learning were considered as having sold their souls to the barbarians in despair of finding any better outlet for their energies."[29]

This is completely different from the attitude of the Japanese to Western studies. The Japanese have always cherished a longing for Western culture, just as they cherished a longing for Chinese culture before it; if there were times when it was not welcome, the reason was not that it was held in contempt, but that it was seen as dangerous. The ultimate reason why the Chinese failed to show any particular curiosity concerning Western civilization lay in their enormous pride in their own. This shows that unlike Japanese society Chinese society was for the most part remote from the world of *amae*. Since the Japanese are sensitive to trends outside their own world and seek at once to identify with or take over whatever seems in any way superior to themselves, contacts with Western culture in their case produced completely different results from that of the Chinese.

Sin and shame

Ever since Ruth Benedict first distinguished two principal cultural patterns based respectively on the sense of guilt and the sense of shame and cited Japanese culture as the typical example of the latter, most foreign students of Japan seem, despite a certain amount of criticism from Japanese scholars, to have accepted her theory. I myself am on the whole disposed to side with her, but more for what we have learned through the sensitivity of her feeling for the Japanese psychology than from any desire to swallow her theories whole. They raise, in fact, a considerable number of questions, not the least of which is the fact that she allows value judgements to creep into her ideas. Specifically, it is evident that when she states that the culture of guilt places emphasis on inner standards of conduct whereas the culture of shame places emphasis on outward standards of conduct she has the feeling that the former is superior to the latter.

A second difficulty is that she seems to postulate guilt and shame as entirely unrelated to each other, which is obviously contrary to the facts. One and the same person very often experiences these two emotions at the same time, and they would seem to have a very close relationship; the person who has committed a "sin" is very frequently ashamed of what he has done. Nevertheless, the impression still remains that in characterizing Japanese culture as a culture of shame she has pointed out something extremely important, and in what follows I shall examine this point in greater detail.[30]

Let us first examine the fact that in Western eyes the Japanese sense of guilt appears to be rather sluggish. The reason is probably that where the Westerner tends to think of the sense of guilt as an inner problem for the individual, the Japanese has no such idea. It would be foolish, of course, to assume that the Japanese have no sense of guilt. What is characteristic about the Japanese sense of guilt, though, is that it shows itself most sharply when the individual suspects that his action will result in betraying the group to which he belongs.

Even with the Western sense of guilt one might, in fact, postulate a deep-lying psychology of betrayal, but the Westerner is not normally conscious of it. What probably happened is that in the course of centuries of exposure to Christian teachings, the group—which almost certainly played an important part in his moral outlook at first—was gradually replaced by God, who in turn faded away with the advent of the modern age, leaving the individual awareness to carry on by itself. Since psychoanalytic opinion holds that the Western sense of guilt arises as a result of going against a super-ego that forms in the inner mind, the element of betrayal would seem not to have disappeared entirely. However, although this super-ego, being defined as a function of the inner mind, may well include individual personal elements such as influences from the parents, its nature is, even so, essentially impersonal. In the Western sense of guilt the sense of betrayal remains only as a trace, and is no longer experienced strongly as such.

With the Japanese, on the other hand, the sense of guilt is most strongly aroused when, as we have seen, the individual betrays the trust of the members of his own group. One could express this differently by saying that the sense of guilt is a function of human relations. For example, in the case of relatives who are most close to him, and parents in particular, the individual does not usually have much sense of guilt, presumably because both sides are so close that *amae* gives confidence of any sin being forgiven. What does often happen, though, is that the sense of guilt hitherto suppressed is felt following a parent's death—as is expressed by the saying that "one realizes one's *on* to one's parents after they are dead."

Generally speaking, the Japanese experience a sense of guilt most frequently in the type of relationship where *giri* is at work and where betrayal could lead to the severing of the link. The word *sumanai*, already dealt with, serves as the most appropriate confession of the sense of guilt in such a case. Moreover, although the sense of guilt as such begins, one might say, when one has done something that one should not, the general view is that there is no admission of one's guilt unless the misdeed is accompanied by a feeling of *sumanai*. The sense of guilt summed up in the word *sumanai* naturally connects up directly with the actual act of apology. The Japanese sense of guilt, thus, shows a very clearcut structure, commencing as it does with betrayal and ending in apology; it represents, in fact, the very prototype of the sense of guilt, and Benedict's failure to see this can only be attributed to her cultural prejudice.

It is very interesting in this connection that Father Heuvers, who has been in Japan ever since the Great Kanto Earthquake of 1923, should have written of his realization of the magical power of the apology in Japan.[31] It is particularly noteworthy that a Christian missionary, who came to Japan to preach forgiveness of sin, should have been so impressed by the realization that among Japanese a heartfelt apology leads easily to reconciliation. I am sure that other foreigners in Japan besides Fr. Heuvers have noticed the same thing, and it may well be this that has given rise to the popular theory that the Japanese have a poor sense of guilt.

An episode that I heard about from an American psychiatrist will also serve to back up the observations of Fr. Heuvers just described. Through some oversight in carrying out immigration formalities, he found himself hauled over the coals by an official of the Immigration Bureau. However often he explained that it was not really his fault, the official would not be appeased until, at the end of his tether, he said "I'm sorry . . ." as a prelude to a further argument, whereupon the official's expression suddenly changed and he dismissed the matter without further ado. The "I'm sorry" that he had used was far from being the same as the Japanese apologetic use of *sumanai*, but the official had obviously taken it as this apologetic *sumanai*. The psychiatrist in question told me this story as an instance of the oddity of the Japanese people, but one might, of course, equally see it as an example of the peculiarity of the Western psychology, since people in the West, despite Benedict's description of them as inhabitants of a culture of guilt—or, one might say a little cynically, precisely because of that—are generally speaking reluctant to apologize. This is something that has gradually come to be recognized as the number of Japanese with experience of travel abroad has increased.[32]

I should like to quote here a story told in an essay by Lafcadio Hearn entitled "At the Railway Station,"[33] which admirably illustrates, I feel, the Japanese attitude towards feelings of guilt. The story begins at the point at which a criminal who, after being arrested for theft, killed a policeman and fled, has been recaptured and brought back to Kumamoto. Facing the crowd that has gathered at the entrance to the station, the officer who has brought him back calls forward the widow of the murdered policeman. She is carrying a small boy on her back. The officer addresses the child. "This is the man who killed your father," he says. The child bursts into tears, whereupon the criminal begins to speak "in a passion of hoarse remorse that made one's heart shake." "Pardon! pardon! pardon me, little one!" he says. "That I did—not for hate was it done, but in mad fear only, in my desire to escape . . . great

51

unspeakable wrong have I done you! But now for my sin I go to die. I wish to die; I am glad to die! Therefore, little one, be pitiful!—forgive me!''

He is led away by the officer, whereupon "quite suddenly the multitude," which hitherto has been listening in complete silence, "began to sob." What is more, there are tears glistening even in the eyes of the policeman who accompanies him.

The scene made a deep impression on Lafcadio Hearn. What struck him as particularly significant was "that the appeal to remorse had been made through the criminal's sense of fatherhood—that potential love of children which is so large a part of the soul of every Japanese." His observation is undoubtedly correct. However, if one carries interpretation one step further, one may surely say that besides feeling sorry for the child the criminal here had also awoken to a sense of his own wretchedness. He was, in a sense, identifying with the child. As I have already pointed out, the word *sumanai* usually includes a plea for the good will of the other party, and the same is true of *mōshiwake nai* (literally, I have no excuse). In other words, it is an expression of a desire to be forgiven even though the relationship as such is not one where *amae* would normally apply. It is this, probably—the way in which, in Japan, an apology comprises what is essentially a child-like plea to the other party, and the fact that this attitude is always received sympathetically—that gives the apology its magical efficacy in foreign eyes. Likewise, the spectators in the story just quoted did not sob just for the child, but for the penitent criminal; in fact, it would probably be more correct to say that in their eyes the images of child and criminal were blended into an inseparable whole. The story, of course, dates from the end of the last century, and nowadays one would very seldom encounter in actuality "human drama" in such a pure form as this. Nevertheless, it seems safe to assume that the same kind of psychology, unconsciously if not consciously, is still at work in the Japanese of today.

Now, if the sense of guilt is something that develops within the self but is directed outward in the form of apology, the sense of shame originates in awareness of the eyes of the outside world and is directed in toward the self. However, there is a close relationship between these two which is illustrated most typically, as I said at the outset, by the case where a sense of guilt is accompanied by a sense of shame. The areas in which the two are experienced are, similarly, overlapping: just as one seldom feels a sense of guilt towards one's innermost circle, so one rarely feels shame. It is the same with strangers with whom one has absolutely no connection—a fact summed up most succinctly in the phrase "the traveler discards his shame." In short, one experiences shame most of all, just as in the case of guilt, in relation to the group to which one belongs; just as betrayal of the group creates guilt, so to be ostracised by the group is the greatest shame and dishonor. For this reason to have a sense of shame is extremely important for someone belonging to a group. The reader of Benedict's *The Chrysanthemum and the Sword* might, incidentally, have the impression that the sense of shame was almost a Japanese monopoly and unknown in the West, but this is of course not so. Even in the West, as early a thinker as Aristotle defined shame as the fear of dishonor, and discussed the position it occupied in the ethical life of man.[34] A subtle difference, however, compared with the traditional Japanese morality, with its emphasis on the sense of shame in men of all ages, is that Aristotle stresses that shame is particularly appropriate to youth.

The reason, incidentally, why foreigners feel that the sense of shame is particularly strong in Japanese would seem to be that in contact with foreigners or when living abroad the Japanese are very often unable to behave freely. The inferiority the

Japanese feel in contact with foreigners is obviously at work here; the desire to be accepted combines with the fear of not being accepted. A proof of this is that the reaction just mentioned is strongest toward Westerners and weak toward other Orientals. Admittedly, today, when Japan's stock has risen in other countries, the Japanese traveler who at one time would have been conscious of himself as a "country cousin" often behaves in other countries in a way that shows only too clearly the accuracy of the saying "the traveler discards his sense of shame," and invites the scorn of foreigners. This seems, however, to be confined to cases where Japanese travel in groups, which almost certainly means that in these cases they feel they are protected by the group and need not be conscious of their surroundings.

This lack of shame when in a group is not, of course, a phenomenon confined to traveling abroad, but is to be found constantly at home in Japan too; indeed, it is perhaps the greatest single characteristic of the Japanese. Generally speaking, the Japanese like group action. It is extremely difficult for a Japanese to transcend the group and act independently. The reason would seem to be that a Japanese feels vaguely that it is treacherous to act on his own without considering the group to which he belongs, and feels ashamed, even, at doing something on his own.

Seen in this light, it becomes clear, I believe, why the sense of shame has in modern times been so lightly dismissed in the West, with its exaltation of independence and self-sufficiency in man. Benedict's definitions of guilt as deriving from an internalization of values and shame as deriving from the criticism of others are an accurate reflection of this trend in the modern Western world. Nevertheless, although to admit to shame may be in itself particularly shameful and thus difficult to practice, the Westerner almost certainly experiences it privately—though, as Erikson[35] points out, there is reason to believe that shame "is early and easily absorbed by guilt." Probably this is because to admit to guilt suits the makeup of the Westerner better in that, more than admitting to shame, it permits him to display his potential power as an individual. One might also say that the sense of shame lies deeper than the sense of sin and guilt.

Among works that have thrown light on this point, there is a fine study by Helen M. Lynd,[36] but I was particularly surprised when I came across the following passage in *Ethics*, a work by the theologian Dietrich Bonhoeffer who was killed by the Nazis during the war: "Shame is man's ineffaceable recollection of his estrangement from the origin; it is grief for this estrangement, and the powerless longing to return to unity with the origin. . . . Shame is more original than remorse."[37]

This view, so much more penetrating than Benedict's superficial views concerning shame, also coincides with the analysis of shame developed in the present work. In Japan, too, Sakuta Keiichi has recently published a work entitled *A Reconsideration of the Culture of Shame*[38] in which he criticizes Benedict's views and emphasizes that the sense of shame is not simply a superficial matter of concern for the good opinion of others but is something extremely delicate, involving the whole inner personality. In practice, the sense of guilt often depends on a feeling that there was no need for one to have done something that one has in fact done. It is, probably, precisely this that makes the Westerner prefer the sense of sin or guilt, for the sense of shame, bringing as it does a sense of the incompleteness and inadequacy of one's own existence as such, is more basic. The man who feels shame must suffer from the feeling of finding himself, his *amae* unsatisfied, exposed to the eyes of those about him when all he wants is to be wrapped warm in his surroundings.

It is interesting that people should be far keener on apologizing in Japan, where the sense of shame is highly developed, than in the West, which is supposed to be a culture of guilt. It is not merely that in Japan the individual says *sumanai* of something that is already done and finished. The Japanese also tend to stress their own lack of power to control what they will do from now on—which is tantamount to an apology, in advance i.e. an excuse. Indeed, the Japanese apology very frequently has, in itself, a ring of self-excuse, a result of the fact that the Japanese sense of guilt includes a considerable admixture of the sense of shame from the very beginning. Generally speaking, the apology *sumanai* is aimed at not losing the other's good will. There is no problem when the feeling of being in the wrong is obviously genuine, but it sometimes happens that the person who repeats *sumanai* with too much facility is rebuffed with the reply *sumanai de sumu to omou ka* (literally, "do you think that to say 'it is not finished' will finish it?" i.e. facile apology is not enough).

Incidentally, the way in which, in Japanese society, some unfortunate occurence or other often leads to the resignation of those connected with the incident out of a "sense of responsibility"—even though there may be, strictly speaking, no individual responsibility—is a typical example of the Japanese confusion of guilt and shame. In such cases, the sense of solidarity with the group to which one belongs takes precedence over true responsibility. Because of this sense of solidarity, the man concerned feels the unhappy occurrence as a disgrace, and cannot see it as unrelated to himself. To do so would be a sin, and shameful as well. From this proceeds the social custom of resigning from one's post as a sign of responsibility, even where none exists in fact; where some circumstance or other makes it impossible to comply with this custom, the individual is tormented indefinitely by his failure. Perhaps the most classic instance of this is the case of General Nogi. During his youth, he was wounded in the Seinan war and had his flag taken from him, unavoidably, by the enemy. He was afforded no suitable opportunity to wipe out the shame, and his sense of shame seems to have been spurred on still further by frequent defeats in battles in which he was involved in later wars. Even so, he was not permitted to withdraw until the very end, and was thus not able to wipe out the accumulated sense of shame until the death of the Emperor Meiji, when he committed suicide in order to follow his lord into death.

The ideology of *amae*

I believe that *amae* was traditionally the Japanese ideology—not in its original sense of "the study of ideas" but in its modern sense of a set of ideas, or leading concept, that forms the actual or potential basis for a whole social system—and still is to a considerable extent today. Not being a sociologist, I do not have the specialist knowledge of the social order or the framework of society necessary to demonstrate this point. It was, in fact, something said by a patient whom I happened to be treating that gave me the first hint, but since then I have become increasingly convinced that what has traditionally been referred to vaguely as the "Japanese spirit" or the "soul of Yamato," as well as more specific "ideologies" such as emperor worship and respect for the emperor system can be interpreted in terms of *amae*.

The hint afforded by one of my patients was as follows. Not long after his treatment had begun, he acquired a new awareness of his own desire to depend on others, and said one day: "When people are children, they depend on their parents, and when they grow up they begin to depend on themselves. Most normal people are the same, I'm sure, but I seem to have gone astray somewhere. I want to depend, but nobody lets me. For the past six months or so, I've been wishing I had someone to act as a mother to me. Someone I could confide anything to, someone who'd take decisions out of my hands. But when you think about it, though that might be all right for me, it would

57

be no fun for the other person. It's the same with you, doctor —I've just been using you lately to unload my gripes on."

The patient here is obviously referring to his unsatisfied desire to *amaeru*. A short while afterwards, he referred to the same feelings again in the following terms: "I want someone to *hohitsu* me. Someone who would leave me to take responsibility to all outward appearances but in fact would give me advice and recognition." *Hohitsu* is a term that can only be translated as "assist," but the point is that "assist" here implies shouldering all actual responsibilities while conceding all apparent authority. The reason for his use of the word, which occurs in the Meiji Constitution and is seldom to be heard in postwar Japan, was probably that he happened himself to be a student of law. At the same time, though, it also showed a considerable psychological insight. By applying to himself a word that was formerly only used of the emperor, he not only gave skillful expression to his own inner desire but also threw light on the psychological significance of the position of the emperor.

The emperor is in a position to expect that those about him will attend to all matters great and small, including, of course, the government of the country. In one sense he is entirely dependent on those about him, yet status-wise it is those about him who are subordinate to the emperor. Where his degree of dependence is concerned, he is no different from a babe in arms, yet his rank is the highest in the land, a fact which is surely proof of the respect accorded infantile dependence in Japan. Another fact suggesting the same kind of principle is that in Japan not only the emperor but all those who stand in high positions have to be bolstered up, as it were, by those about them. In other words, it is the person who can embody infantile dependence in its purest form who is most qualified to stand at the top in Japanese society. This is backed up by the praise traditionally accorded to *sunaosa* (guilelessness, straightforwardness, amenability) as the highest of the virtues. The fact, pointed out by Benedict, that in Japan the greatest freedom and self-indulgence is accorded to infants and the elderly is also, probably, related to this. This last point, admittedly, may have changed somewhat with the increasing complexity of society nowadays, but it seems that the tendency still survives to a considerable degree.

As the preceding paragraphs will suggest, the description of the emperor in the postwar constitution as a "symbol of the Japanese nation" is peculiarly apt. In the old Meiji Constitution, the corresponding description is "sacred and inviolable." This may have more solemn and religious overtones than the description in the new constitution, yet there is, surely, no essential discrepancy between the two. The almost religious character that the Meiji Constitution came to acquire seems, incidentally, to have been influenced by the fact that Itō Hirobumi, its drafter, perceived that religion lay at the foundation of constitutional government in Europe. Itō himself, during debate in the Privy Council on the draft of the Imperial Constitution, referred to this fact, and declared that apart from the Imperial family there was little to serve as a spiritual focus for constitutional government in Japan.[38]

In short, he treated the Imperial family as a kind of spiritual substitute for Christianity. Whatever the rights or wrongs of the matter, his view that the traditional religions were useless for his purpose, and that the only thing that could help in binding the nation spiritually was the ancient concept of the nation as a family, with the Imperial family as its main branch, was undoubtedly wise in its way. Historical research, of course, has shown that the Japanese Imperial family were themselves conquerors who came from abroad in ancient times, yet the fact that in subsequent history the Imperial family served as the spiritual center of society is undeniable; and, moreover, since the beginning of the Tokugawa regime or even earlier the spirit of resistance to the authority of the time invariably used the Imperial family as its starting point. To express it from a different angle, the Imperial family, as *ōyake*, served—as I have pointed out already in the section on "inner" and "outer" circles—as a kind of substitute for the public spirit in the Western sense even before the promulgation of the Meiji Constitution. It seems likely that in Japanese society, which so easily splits up into any number of closed circles, there existed no appropriate and effective concept that could unify the whole nation apart from that of being "His Majesty's children."

The Japanese, in short, idealized *amae* and considered a world dominated by *amae* as a truly human world; and the emperor system might be seen as an institutionalization of this idea. The theories of *kokutai goji* ("preserving the body politic") of which so much was heard following the Meiji Restoration were not simply invented for the political convenience of the ruling class, but were also backed up by the desire to preserve this Japanese view of the world in the face of pressure from outside. And the Pacific War was fought in the cause of extending this view of the world to countries overseas as well. It is true of course that until the final utter defeat in war and the complete loss by the Japanese of confidence in the ideas of "national polity" and "Japanese spirit" that had been their support hitherto, they were not allowed to consider, even, what was the essence of the emperor system. Shortly after the end of the war, Maruyama Masao is said to have summed up the emperor system as a system of irresponsibility, yet even though he may have perceived this in prewar days the fact remains that defeat was necessary before it was possible for him to make his views public, nor would the patient whom I previously quoted have dreamed before the end of the war of using about himself the word *hohitsu*, a term normally employed only about the emperor.

The question, however, is not restricted to the emperor system in the narrow sense. So long as concepts such as *giri*, *ninjō*, repaying one's obligations (*hōon*), or even "the soul of Yamato" remained active as controlling influences in society, it was impossible to perceive that, essentially, these all derived from the *amae* psychology. It was not until the emperor himself denied the myths and became the "symbol" of the Japanese people that it became possible to bring into the light the *amae* lurking in the heart of each individual Japanese.

The present age has seen the collapse of the emperor system as an ideology. As a result, uncontrolled *amae* has, as it were, run rampant and "little emperors" have sprung up here, there, and everywhere. This does not mean, however, that everything in the nature of a system has disappeared; and recently, partly as a result of Japan's re-emergence as a great economic power, there has even been talk of a "revival." I should like to devote some space here to the social customs that seem, along with the emperor system, to have supported the ideology of *amae*.

First of all, there is the use of honorific language, which is extremely highly developed in Japanese. Honorific language, as the word suggests, is used in order to show respect or defer- ence towards someone of superior station to oneself, but what is certain is that the man toward whom it is used feels a sense of pleasure rather than any sense that he is being kept at a respectful distance. It occurred to me that there was a very strong resemblance in Japanese between the honorific language used towards superiors and the way people talk to children. For example, a woman might say to someone else's small boy *botchan wa o-rikō-san desu ne* (What a clever boy), the word *rikō* (clever) being given two honorifics, the prefix *o-* and the suffix *-san*. Or she might say to a small girl *O-jō-chan no o-yōfuku wa kirei desu ne* (Your dress is pretty, isn't it. What a pretty dress!). Here, the phrase corresponding to the English "your" employs a term used of someone else's daughter and itself incorporating

61

an honorific prefix and suffix (an idea of the flavor might be given by translating it "little miss's"), while even the word for dress has its honorific prefix.

Considering this lavish use of the honorific prefix in addressing children, I came to wonder if the aim in using honorific language to superiors might not be to humor them in the same way that it is used to humor children. Generally speaking, failure to use honorifics to one's superiors means putting them out of temper and eventually placing oneself at a disadvantage. But the fact that it is necessary at all to "butter up" one's superiors in the same way as one does children is evidence, surely, of the persistence of a childlike attitude in Japanese adults. This also coincides with Benedict's view, already cited, that in Japan the greatest degree of freedom and self-indulgence is permitted to children and the elderly.

The next question I should like to glance at is that of ancestor worship. This custom is not, of course, confined to Japan, yet the peculiar tenacity of ancestor worship there is witnessed by the fact that Buddhism, despite the great popularity that it once appeared to enjoy in Japan, gained a hold on the general masses less for its ideas than as a form of ancestor worship. Now, the connection between popular ideas of "dying and becoming a god" or "dying and becoming a Buddha" and the *amae* psychology was first brought home to me through my own personal experience. Following the death in rapid succession of both my parents and the consequent severing of my bonds with them, I became aware of them for the first time as independent *persons*, where hitherto their existence was real to me only insofar as they were my own parents. This made me wonder whether to become a god or a Buddha for the Japanese might not mean that human personality of the individual concerned, which during his lifetime had frequently been lost sight of, buried beneath formal relationships or plastered over with the cares of everyday life, was accorded new attention and respect. This in no respect contradicts the traditional belief that considered the emperor the embodiment of satisfied *amae*, as a god incarnate. Indeed, one might well see ancestor worship as existing in a mutually complementary relationship with emperor worship, since both use the term "god" in referring to those who lie in the realm beyond the anguish of unsatisfied *amae*—which is where, this suggests, the essence of the Japanese concept of divinity lies.

Finally, I would like to add something concerning the Japanese fondness for festivals. The Japanese have a passion for them; in the large towns, the festivals held for the gods of local shrines or in honor of ancestors seem to have fallen into abeyance, yet even the town dweller still seizes every slightest excuse for creating a "festival" and going on a spree. The object of the festival does not have to be a god or human being of old; anything at all special or commemorable, whether an event, a thing, or some newly inaugurated social system, will serve as an excuse.

This can obviously be interpreted as a manifestation of the traditional Shinto spirit; the point has been discussed by many scholars already, and I hardly need to go into it here. One suggestion I would like to make, however, concerns the relationship between the festival habit and the feelings expressed in the closely related word *medetai*, usually translated as "auspicious" or "happy." Philologically speaking, this is connected with the verb *mederu* and means something like "worthy of being appreciated or enjoyed." Originally it probably expressed a feeling of admiration for the thing being celebrated, but nowadays it has come to indicate chiefly the gay, "auspicious" feeling of festival time. The Japanese love of festivals might equally appropriately be described as a love of the *medetai* feeling. What is still more interesting is that nowadays the word *medetai* is frequently used in what would not be considered *medetai* contexts: for example, "He's a little *medetai*," means "He's rather

63

soft" in the sense of easily put upon, easily moved to unnecessary gratitude, admiration, etc. This usage seems to be comparatively new, and does not appear in the old *Daigenkai* dictionary. From this, I believe, one might infer that in olden times the Japanese were able to indulge in the *medetai* feeling quite simply and unsophisticatedly, but that in recent years what was once *medetai* has gradually become less so. This is probably related to the fact that the ideology of *amae* in the sense described earlier has collapsed, with a corresponding decline in the market value of *amae*, so that the man who quite happily continues to *amaeru* (i.e. assume the goodwill of others) is described as *medetai*. In practice, it might be truer not to confine the expression to a few particular individuals but to say that the Japanese as a whole are, without realizing it, *medetai*, since despite the collapse of the *amae* ideology the individual Japanese has not proved able to deny the *amae* in his heart of hearts.

3 The logic of *amae*

Language and psychology

In describing, in chapter two, the way in which Japanese society has created a world permeated by *amae*, my method relied to a large extent—for example, in taking the vocabulary of *amae* as the starting-point for discussion—on the semantic analysis of words. It was not semantics pure and simple, being backed up by comparative linguistic observation, yet it differed somewhat from what is normally known as comparative linguistics. It was based on the premise that each of the various languages of the world expresses its own unique world of meaning, and that it is possible to draw certain conclusions from a comparison of these worlds. Of course, I was not conscious of this premise from the very outset of my studies; as I said in chapter one, I originally came to realize the importance of the concept of *amae* gradually, through a combination of my own personal experience and my clinical experience as a psychiatrist, plus an examination of those experiences by psychoanalytical methods. It was this that led me to make *amae* the central focus of my studies. In doing so, I was seeking to use the concept as a methodology in ascertaining the true nature of various types of psychopathology, but at the same time I became convinced that the world of meaning centering around that concept represented the true essence of the Japanese psychology.

This latter conclusion is based on the premise that national character must be reflected in the national language. Thinking to find out what the experts had to say on this subject, I read a work by the linguist Edward Sapir.[40] I was somewhat disappointed to find my premise clearly rejected. But specialist though Sapir was, I was already too taken with my concept of *amae* to submit to him meekly. Applying the principles of the methods I used constantly as a psychiatrist, I reasoned in the following fashion. Clinical psychiatry is based on the assumption that it is possible to get to know a patient's mental state via the words that he uses. If this assumption is correct in the case of an individual, surely it should also be true of a nation that speaks one uniform language. Surely it should be possible to discuss the psychological characteristics of a people in terms of the language it speaks.

I later found that this view was not only mine, but was held by a number of different scholars. The philosopher Ernst Cassirer, for example, has the following to say: "(Names) are not designed to refer to substantial things, independent entities which exist by themselves. They are determined rather by human interests and human purposes. But these interests are not fixed and invariable. . . . For in the act of denomination we select, out of the multiplicity and diffusion of our sense data, certain fixed centers of perception."[41] He quotes Goethe's celebrated saying, "He who knows no foreign language does not know his own," and cites an example given by Wilhelm von Humboldt, who believed that words give shape to and determine our spiritual lives. As Humboldt sees it, the Greek (*mēn*) and Latin (*luna*) words for moon show different types of interest in the moon. The former, he says, treats the moon as a means of measuring the passage of time, while the latter expresses the moon's brightness.

I also learned that Benjamin L. Whorf, the American linguist, had expressed, independently, essentially the same views as those just quoted. The following passage sums up his views on the subject. "Actually, thinking is most mysterious, and by far the greatest light upon it that we have is thrown by the study of language. This study shows that the forms of a person's thoughts are controlled by inexorable laws of pattern of which he is unconscious. These patterns are the unperceived intricate systematizations of his own language—shown readily enough by a candid comparison and contrast with other languages, especially those of a different linguistic family. His thinking itself is in a language—in English, in Sanskrit, in Chinese. And every language is a vast pattern-system, different from others, in which are culturally ordained the forms and categories by which the personality not only communicates, but also analyzes nature, notices or neglects types of relationship and phenomena, channels his reasoning, and builds the house of his consciousness."[42]

Whorf believes that it is especially profitable to compare languages belonging to different families; in this sense, a comparison of Japanese and the languages of the West is surely peculiarly suitable. The present work, of course, is not concerned with an overall comparison, but almost exclusively with the single word *amae*. Nevertheless, the word in question refers to the basic human relationships, and has, moreover, a rich associated vocabulary that expresses all the many variations on the psychology summed up by *amae* and that clearly forms one broad pattern. If, then, there is nothing corresponding to it in the languages of the West, one must conclude that there is an obvious difference between the Westerner and the Japanese in their views of the world and their apprehension of reality.

Let us at this point delve a little more deeply into the relationship between language and thought. Without doubt, different languages seem to express different types of awareness of reality, and in this respect a language can be said to condition, to some extent, the thinking of those who use it. Nevertheless, it would be a mistake to conclude from this that thought depends entirely on language and that thought without language is impossible. The very fact that we can understand that different languages express different worlds of significance is, in itself, a sign that thought essentially transcends language. Of course, the statement that thought transcends language is in itself a verbal expression, and it remains impossible for human beings to express thought without using words, yet the essence of thought as such transcends the verbal expression of it.

To say this is to consider thought from the viewpoint of logic—that is, from the viewpoint of understanding the sense—but even when one considers thought from the viewpoint of psychology it seems a natural conclusion that it has its origins prior to words. For instance, if, as I claim in this book, the vocabulary of *amae* is something unique, then it is possible to explain its occurence in psychological terms. And the psychological explanation thus postulated must assume a psychological process which precedes words. To put it more simply, the fact that the word *amae* exists in Japanese whereas nothing corresponding to it exists in Western languages can be interpreted as meaning that the Japanese are particularly sensitive to *amae* and set great store by it, whereas Westerners are not and do not, and to explain this one must obviously consider the psychological processes which precede words.

Considered linguistically, what I have just pointed out relates to the philological origins of individual words, but in terms of psychoanalysis it concerns the link between words as such and unconscious psychological processes. Let us turn our attention for a while, then, to the psychoanalytic understanding of words. Freud himself made the highly pregnant statement that "... in men there is an added complication owing to which internal processes in the ego may also acquire the quality of consciousness. This complication is produced by the function of speech, which brings the material in the ego into a firm connection with the memory-traces of visual and more particularly of auditory perceptions."[43] This point is made still more explicit in the following quotation from Rapaport: "The memorial connections, the conceptual belongingness, and the anticipations which have once arisen in the interplay of motivations and the quest for the object which satisfies simultaneously several effective motives (over-determination) are not lost with the progress of psychological development; rather, by again and again recurring in approximately similar situations, they become structuralized and available as fixed tools, quasi-stationary apparatuses, for use in the thought process."[44] Rapaport does not specifically refer to words here, but it seems safe to take "fixed tools, quasi-stationary apparatuses, for use in the thought process" as referring to words or to the stage immediately preceding them. If so, then this passage can be said to describe how words reflect the state of affairs in the early stages of psychological development, i.e. the way in which the individual relates to his surroundings via his desires.

Words, now, do not merely reflect unselectively every aspect of the situation during the early stages of psychological development. Selection invariably takes place; some things are dealt with in language, but other things, it would seem, cannot be, and are therefore banished from the consciousness. If language determines thought to a certain extent as Whorf says, then it is probably because of this fact. The determining occurs as a result of a particular person being born in a particular linguistic society, but ultimately it derives from decisions made as the language was originally coming into being. Admittedly, these two things are not necessarily different, and one might say that every time a human being acquires a language the birth of language is repeated afresh on an individual basis.

It was the psychoanalyst S. L. Kubie who first paid attention to the choice that occurs in the process of a language's coming into being, or of acquiring a language. "The neurotic process is always a symbolic process: and the split into parallel yet interacting streams of conscious and unconscious processes

69

starts approximately as the child begins to develop the rudiments of speech. This rudimentary speech is at first a language of action and not of words; but there is good reason to believe that the evolution of the capacity to use language is linked closely to the process by which we first repress and then represent our unconscious struggles."[45]

Since this quotation is difficult to understand in isolation, I should like to explain in a little more detail with reference to a paper published later by Kubie.[46] The "symbolic process" of which he speaks is a comprehensive term comprising linguistic activity in the broadest sense, and not merely symbols in the narrow sense in which the term is used in psychoanalysis. Symbols in the narrow sense are, principally, those that appear in dreams or psychopathological phenomena, in cases where they represent psychological processes of which the individual himself is not aware. Kubie uses the term symbolic process to cover both these and normal verbal activities, since he believes that there is a developmental connection between the two. According to his theory, all symbolic representatives have two points of reference, one internal with respect to the boundaries of the body (the constellation "I"), and one external (the constellation "Non-I"). Where such representatives take the form of speech, it is the "Non-I" constellation on which the emphasis is normally placed, the I here being frequently ignored. In other words, he says, there is a tendency for representatives relating to one's own physical sensations to be repressed in the course of language development. The question, now, is why, in transforming representatives into language, the emphasis should be on the "Non-I"; this is probably attributable ultimately to the fact that the exterior world is vital to the survival of the individual. The apparent emphasis placed on the "Non-I" can be seen as directed, ultimately, by the interest of the self. Interest here, even so, means principally interest in survival, so that representatives related to other physical sensations of the self are sacrificed, and it seems likely that the desires and impulses that these represent are repressed at this point, giving rise to unconscious conflicts. These unconscious conflicts later make themselves apparent as dreams and psychopathological phenomena, which is the point at which representatives related to one's own physical sensations appear as symbols in the narrow sense.

This theory of Kubie's was made in order to explain language in general and the relation between language and psychopathology in particular, and not to explain the differences that occur between different languages. Nevertheless, his theory that all symbolic processes have, essentially, "I" and "Non-I" offers a likely hypothesis for explaining the origins of the variety observable in different languages. This could be seen as a further extension of Cassirer's theory that names are determined by human interests and aspirations, and the theory of Whorf that language presents the patterns of unconscious thought. For the question of which aspects of the "Non-I" are emphasized and which aspects of the "I" ignored in the formation of language implies a choice of one among many different possibilities—which is precisely, it would seem, where the seeds of the peculiarity of individual languages take shape. In attempting to explain the relationship between linguistic activity and emotion the philosopher Susan Langer,[47] who carried on the work of Cassirer, states that language, by abstracting certain emotions from among the bewildering wealth and variety that exist, seeks to make them effective, which is surely, in essence, the same as what Kubie has to say. Either way, the point is that language is not merely a means for human beings to express their emotions but in its very forms bears the imprint of the human psychology.

The verbal origins of *amae*

Seen in the light of its present usage, and of its development as a word, *amae* naturally evokes associations with the behavior of an infant in its relationship with its mother, yet oddly enough the leading Japanese dictionaries make no mention of this. *Daigenkai*, for instance, says simply, "to lean on a person's good will," and the examples given all concern adults; not one concerns infants. This may imply that our awareness of *amae* as something essentially infantile is, chronologically, comparatively recent and that no attention at all was paid to this in the past. One must inquire, then, what associations this word had in the minds of the Japanese who first used it, which resolves into the question of the derivation of the word *amae* itself. I can find nothing on this subject in any existing work.

In what follows I shall take my courage in both hands and speculate as an amateur. First, I suspect that *ama*, the root of the word *amae*, may be related to the childish word *uma-uma* indicating the child's request for the breast or food, which is the first word that almost all Japanese speak. *Daigenkai* recognizes that *amashi* (sweet) can have the same sense as *umashi* (pleasant-tasting), which makes my fancied connection between *ama* and the *uma* of *uma-uma* still more likely. If this fancy is correct, the *ama* of *amae*, philologically speaking, is related to infancy. If so, then it is only natural that we should now have come to consider *amae* as a particularly infantile phenomenon, but to the ancients who first created the word intellectual judgements such as the distinction between infant and adult were of course irrelevant. They would surely have attached more importance to the feeling contained in the word. As to what precisely this feeling was, I believe that the most correct answer would be the sense of longing expressed in the desire for the breast. The ancients, of course, almost certainly did not experience this emotion solely as a desire for the breast, but felt the same type of longing for anything that conferred benefits on them. This has led me to wonder—rashly, perhaps—whether the *ama* of *amae* cannot be identified in turn with the *ama* meaning the heavens and the *ama* that came to be used as a *makura-kotoba*.* I feel this because the heavens for the ancient Japanese seem not to have been something to be feared, something separate from the earth, but something that chiefly conferred blessings on man.

In a discussion on "The Japanese and Japanese Thinking"[48] held recently by Izumi Seiichi, Inoue Mitsutada and Umesao Tadao, the participants discussed the "heaven" of the Japanese as something "continuous" as opposed to the "separate" heaven of the nomadic peoples. This accords very well with what I have just explained. In fact, expressions such as *amakudaru* and *amagakeru*** that are still used frequently today are to be found already in the *Kojiki* and *Manyōshū*, two of the earliest written works in the language. Amaterasu Ōmikami, the Sun Goddess who was believed to be the ancestress of the Japanese nation, is for the most part an extremely maternal, human goddess. This suggests that the origins of *amae* and the myth of the Sun Goddess spring from the same roots, which, if true, would be very intriguing.

---

* A device much used in ancient Japanese poetry. Consisting of groups of syllables (often five in number) always found prefixed to particular nouns or names, they had in many cases already lost much of their meaning and served as pure embellishments or as a way of filling out the meter.
** Literally, "to descend from heaven" and "to ascend to heaven," nowadays used ironically in reference to government officials who use their influence to obtain posts for themselves in private organizations, or of executives in private business who move up into government circles.

The psychological prototype of *amae*

It is obvious that the psychological prototype of *amae* lies in the psychology of the infant in its relationship to its mother. A few observations, then, on this point: first, it is interesting that no one says of a newly born child that it is *amaeru*-ing. A child is not said to *amaeru* until, in the latter half of the year following its birth, it first begins to become aware of its surroundings and to seek after its mother.

Amae, in other words, is used to indicate the seeking after the mother that comes when the infant's mind has developed to a certain degree and it has realized that its mother exists independently of itself. In other words, until it starts to *amaeru* the infant's mental life is an extension, as it were, of its life in the womb, and the mother and child are still unseparated. However, as its mind develops it gradually realizes that itself and its mother are independent existences, and comes to feel the mother as something indispensable to itself; it is the craving for close contact thus developed that constitutes, one might say, *amae*.

In principle, now, this phenomenon should be observable in all human babies, whether in the East or in the West. Nor is it confined to humans; even among animals the unweaned young cling to their mother, so that it is possible to say for instance that a puppy *amaerus* to its mother. The characteristic of human beings, however, is that the psychological content of this type of action can be observed, and the invention in Japanese of the word *amae* in particular has helped in bringing this psychology into closeup. The concept, in short, serves as a medium making it possible for the mother to understand the infant mind and respond to its needs, so that mother and child can enjoy a sense of commingling and identity. What is more,

74

it has had the effect, among the Japanese who are much more aware of *amae* than the peoples who do not possess such a word, of permitting the *amae* psychology to exert a strong influence on every aspect of man's spiritual life—and has also made necessary, it seems, a correspondingly large vocabulary to indicate the variations of the *amae* psychology. It was thus that, as we have already seen in chapter one, the world of *amae* came about.

Now if, as I have stated, the prototype of *amae* is the infant's desire to be close to its mother, who, it has come vaguely to realize, is a separate existence from itself, then one may perhaps describe *amae* as, ultimately, an attempt psychologically to deny the fact of separation from the mother. Obviously enough, the mother and child following birth are separate existences both physically and psychologically. Despite this, the *amae* psychology works to foster a sense of oneness between mother and child. In this sense, the *amae* mentality could be defined as the attempt to deny the fact of separation that is such an inseparable part of human existence and to obliterate the pain of separation. It is also possible to reason that wherever the *amae* psychology is predominant the conflicts and anxiety associated with separation are, conversely, lurking in the background.

This does not imply, of course, that *amae* is necessarily always non-realistic and defensive. Without *amae*, in fact, it is impossible to establish the mother-child relationship and without the mother-child relationship the proper growth of the child would be impossible. Even after adulthood, in the forming of new human relationships, *amae* is invariably at work at least at the very outset. Thus *amae* plays an indispensable role in a healthy spiritual life. If it is unrealistic to close one's eyes completely to the fact of separation, it is equally unrealistic to be overwhelmed by it and isolate oneself in despair over the possibilities of human relationships.

Amae and Japanese thinking

Scholars have put forward many different theories concerning the ways of thinking of the Japanese, but most agree in the long run that, compared with thought in the West, it is not logical but intuitive. I believe that this is not unrelated to the dominance in Japan of the *amae* mentality, since there is something typically illogical from the outset in the attempt to deny the fact of separation and generate, mainly by emotional means, a sense of identity with one's surroundings.

As a result of his comparative studies of Oriental ways of thinking, Nakamura Hajime has stated[49] that an outstanding trend in Japanese thought is the importance attached to closed ethical organizations. This, too, may be interpreted as referring, in different terms, to the *amae* mentality. The same is true of the *shiteki nikō* ("private binomial formula") which Mori Arimasa[50] has recently proposed as a characteristic of Japanese thought. These terms such as "exclusive," "private" and so on used to describe Japanese characteristics are all, I would point out, applicable only when the world of *amae* is viewed from the outside: the inhabitants of that world are themselves quite lacking in any sense that it is either exclusive or private. If anything, they consider themselves to be open and non-exclusive. As we saw in chapter one, it is true that "others" (*tanin*), so long as they remain others, stand outside the world of *amae*, in which sense there does exist exclusivism of a kind. Yet seen in a different way this world also has the function of seeking to "melt down" others by *amae* and make them lose their *tanin* quality, in which sense one might almost call it all-embracing and inclusivist. Even so, to persons on the outside who do not appreciate *amae* the conformity imposed by the world of *amae* is intolerable, so that it seems exclusivist and private, or even egocentric.

To look at the world of *amae* in a negative and criticial way is to see it as irrational, exclusivist, and private, but viewed more positively it can also be seen as respecting nondiscrimination and equality, and as very tolerant. It seems to me, for example, that Zen *satori* (enlightenment) as expounded by the late Suzuki Daisetsu might be interpreted as a positive affirmation of this type of *amae*. I hasten to add that by "affirmation of *amae*" I do not mean merely the permitting and encouraging of *amae*, but the gathering up and setting in a beneficial direction of all the potentials it comprises. Thus it may seem on the surface sometimes to transcend *amae*. The Zen question "what did one look like before one's mother and father were born?" would seem to be getting at this point. The stress on the indivisibility of subject and object, or of the self and others, is also basically the same.

However, since human existence is ultimately dependent on the parents, it is not possible to eliminate the father and mother, however much one may achieve enlightenment through Zen. There occurs a turning back to the mother and father—though this trend may, admittedly, be particularly prominent in the Zen thought of Japan. A Zen priest once said that Zen *satori* could be summed up in the word filial piety, while Suzuki Daisetsu points out that whereas "at the basis of the ways of thinking and feeling of the Westerner there is the father," it is the mother that lies at the bottom of the Oriental nature. "The mother," he says, "enfolds everything in an unconditional love. There is no question of right or wrong. Everything is accepted without difficulties or questioning. Love in the West always contains a residue of power. Love in the East is all-embracing. It is open to all sides. One can enter from any direction.[51] One might see this as nothing other than a eulogy to *amae*.

This spirit of non-discrimination and equality, I believe, has been a part of the Japanese makeup ever since ancient times, and not merely as part of Zen ideas. I believe in fact, that the so-called "way of the Gods" is precisely that, since the "way of the Gods" seems consistently to have extolled the principle of no-principle and the value of no-value. It is this policy, in fact, that has allowed the Japanese to devour various alien cultures without any particular sign of indigestion and to make them, in some fashion or other, their own. From a bystander's viewpoint this may seem to indicate a total lack of ideas or integrity. It is this that Maruyama Masao refers to [52] in speaking of the lack of any "axis of coordinates" as the characteristic of Japanese thought. This view, however, arises from taking other countries as one's model; the Japanese, in fact, have got by perfectly well. One Japanese, Motoori Norinaga, for example, gave this Japanese attitude his whole-hearted approbation: "Everything, the good and the bad alike, is the work of the gods; thus teachings such as Confucianism, Buddhism, and Taoism are alike the work of the gods, and so is the fact that men are led astray by them. It is in this sense that distinctions of good and bad, right and wrong, exist. Confucianism, Buddhism and Taoism are all, in the broadest sense, the Way of the Gods of their respective ages. . . . It follows that in governing a country one should first of all try to ensure safety from harm by behaving in accordance with the will of the benevolent gods as did the ancients, but if it should prove difficult to rule without resort to Confucianism one should rule through Confucianism. If only Buddhism will meet the requirements of the age, one should rule through Buddhism. For they are all, in their own time, the Way of the Gods. On the other hand, to believe that one should apply the ways of the ancients to the government of later ages in every respect is to set the power of man above that of the gods; not only is this impossible, it is contrary to the Way of the Gods of that time . . . Since, therefore, it is beyond the power of man, one should resign oneself to doing what seems best at any given moment."[53]

It seems that if one tries the positive approach to Japanese thinking, one inevitably ends up accepting the "way of the Gods." However, of this I shall have more to say later. In the meantime, let us give some thought to the Japanese aesthetic sense.

In this sphere too, the *amae* sensibility seems to play a very large role. "Beauty" usually implies that an object is pleasing to the senses, the person who enjoys the beauty of the object becoming one with it through that experience. This has much in common with the experience of *amae*, since *amae* itself, as we have frequently seen already, seeks to achieve identity with another. Of course, it is absolutely essential in the latter case that the other person should understand one's purpose and acquiesce in it. Since this is not always possible, the person who seeks *amae* often experiences frustration, and even when he is satisfied the satisfaction does not usually last indefinitely. It is for this reason, it would seem, that some people turn to Zen and other religions, and the same motivation, it seems, also drives some people to the pursuit of beauty. One not uncommonly sees, among those who pursue beauty, persons who are themselves strongly aware of an unsatisfied *amae* and for that reason devote themselves still more intently to the quest for beauty. The fact that the Japanese as a whole are more aesthetically inclined than other peoples may be based on the same reason: if one dwells continuously in the world of *amae* so that the *amae* sensibility is subject to constant stimulation, one becomes obliged, it would seem, to seek beauty whether one wishes it or not.

The first thing that comes to mind in this connection is the spirit of *sabi* and *wabi*, those celebrated ingredients of the Japanese aesthetic sense. Both *wabi* and *sabi* imply a type of quietism that shuns the world of men, and as such would seem

79

to be diametrically opposed to the desire for human contact dominated by *amae*. Yet the person who has achieved the desired state of tranquillity does not fence off his solitude but experiences a strange sense of identity with his surroundings. It is possible too, via this state of mind, to achieve new contact with others of like mind.

Another important concept—one that stands, as it were, in contrast to *wabi* and *sabi*—is that of *iki* (approximations are flair, wit, stylishness). Unlike *wabi* and *sabi*, this is not achieved by divorcing oneself from the world of men, but may be described as the aesthetic sense of the man who lives in the humdrum world yet purges life of the clumsiness and ugliness that often goes with *amae* in its cruder manifestations. The "ugliness" of *amae* refers to the sulkiness, resentment and other warped feelings arising from frustrated *amae*, which often keep a person in a prison from which he cannot escape; the *iki* man, being well versed in the ways of the world, has his wits about him and when the occasion requires can show a *savoir-faire* that arouses the admiration of those about him.

In *Iki no Kōzō* (The Structure of *Iki*), a fine work by Kuki Shūzō which discusses *iki* in detail, the author defines *iki* as "free from loutishness, sophisticated," "an attractiveness that is completely sophisticated, resilient, and free of flabbiness," then touches on the relationship between it and the *amae* mentality.[54] He does not refer to *amae* as a specifically Japanese quality in the sense in which we are dealing with it in the present work. Nevertheless, he takes the position that "*iki* is one of the outstanding self-manifestations of the peculiar mode of being of the Japanese," and in the course of trying to explain it touches on the relationship with the *amae* mentality, thereby giving additional backing to the thesis of the present work. *Iki* he says, together with *shibumi* (literally, astringency or tartness) and *amami* (literally, sweetness), are special heterosexual modes of being ... taking *amami* as the normal state, there is a path that leads via *iki*, where one begins to show some restraint in one's attitude toward others, to *shibumi*. Concerning such *amami*, he explains it as the mood that is revealed in phrases, such as *amaeru sugata iro fukashi* (a woman is most desirable when she *amaeru*s).

It is most interesting that he makes no mention here of the infantile origins of this *amae*, but interprets it mainly as a function of relations between the sexes. This may be partly due to the fact that the literature he refers to in *Iki no Kōzō* is mostly literature of the Edo period, yet it can also be because Kuki himself did not recognize the infantile nature of *amae*. Or he may have realized it yet have been unwilling to admit it in discussing its relevance to something so closely connected with sexual attraction as *iki*. Either way, this would seem to bear out the fact that, as I have already suggested in passing, awareness of the infantile nature of *amae* is of very recent standing. Since Kuki's work was first published in 1930, one may conclude that, if his associations corresponded with those of the average Japanese, *amae* in the ordinary person's mind was, at least until that time, associated with relations between the sexes rather than with child psychology.

Nothing, probably, can be said with accuracy on this score unless one goes further afield and examines the use of *amae* in novels and other works written between the Meiji Restoration and the present day. For example, almost the only case I can find in which Natsume Sōseki uses the word is in connection with the relation between husband and wife, which tends to support what I have already said. The case in question occurs at the beginning of the novel *Meian*, when the character Tsuda has a conversation with his wife concerning the fact that the date suddenly fixed for his operation coincides with a day at the theater to which they have been invited by relatives. His wife says that she does not like to turn down the relatives when they have been so kind, while Tsuda says that it does not matter since the circumstances are beyond their control, whereupon the wife says, "But I *want* to go." "Go if you want to, then," replies Tsuda. "Then why don't you come too?" asks his wife, "Don't you want to?" The feelings this arouses in Tsuda are described as follows: "Raising his eyes to look at his wife, he was struck momentarily by a kind of strange power lurking in his wife's gaze. Her eyes had an odd gleam quite at variance with the mild (*amae*) turns of phrase she had been using. About to reply to what she had said, his mind found its working momentarily interrupted by the expression of those eyes. But almost immediately she smiled, showing her fine white teeth. And at the same moment, the expression in her eyes vanished without trace." Her next remark is, "Don't worry. I don't particularly care about going to the theater, I just wanted to endear myself to you (*amaeru*)."

I have discussed some of the characteristics of Japanese thinking in their relation to the *amae* mentality, but one could doubtless find connections in all kinds of other spheres. For example, the celebrated *mononoaware* cited by Motoori Norinaga (sensitivity to beauty, the "ah-ness of things") would seem to be related to the *amae* sensibility. *Aware* is to be moved by a certain object, whether it be a human being or something in nature, and quietly and profoundly to make oneself one with that object. One might even say that ultimately both *wabi* and *sabi*, as well as *iki* and even the approach to human relations formalized in the concepts of *giri* and *ninjō*, are rooted originally in *mononoaware*. And if one traced this back further still, one would arrive at the primal experience of the Japanese in ancient times.

This primal experience gave rise, on the one hand, to the emperor system and the family-centered society that is related to it, and, on the other, fostered the peculiarly Japanese ways of feeling and thinking. Now I would suggest that the basic emotional urge that has fashioned the Japanese for two thousand years is none other than the *amae* mentality. The realization that this mentality, as has already been suggested several times, is basically childish did not, I suspect, occur to anyone until after Japan's defeat in World War II. If, as I believe, this is so, then the fact could be explained in the following fashion.

First, the men of old did not of course distinguish their primal experience as "primitive" or "childish," but experienced it simply as emotion. And it might well be imagined that Japan's isolation as an island country meant that while, with the passage of time, the emotion embodied in the primal experience might be refined, it was preserved with relatively little change until later ages. Despite her isolation Japan was subject, of course, to various cultural influences from other countries, and this gradually prompted an awareness of Japan's own peculiar culture. This was why, from the time of Motoori Norinaga onward, there was so much talk of the "way of the Gods"—in spite of the fact that this is the "way" beyond words—and it was doubtless for the same reason that there was so much discussion of the "national polity" following the Meiji Restoration. A similar reason probably lay behind the popular spread of Zen, following the Meiji Restoration, among the general public. It is interesting in this connection that the "Nishida philosophy" that won such a following in prewar Japan should, in its emphasis on the pure experience in which subject and object merge, have been so obviously influenced by Zen, since Nishida* himself was firmly convinced that his philosophy, while inspired by the traditions of Western philosophy, was rooted in the Japanese experience.[55]

It would seem, now, that the realization that the essence of the Japanese experience lies in the period of infancy was not possible until, as we have seen in the section on "The Ideology of *Amae*," the shock of defeat undermined the authority of the

---

* Nishida Kitaro (1870–1945), a philospher and student of Japanese culture who expounded a peculiarly Japanese, eclectic philosophy centering around the concept of *mu*, "void."

moral concepts that had bound together Japanese society so far. When people amidst the havoc wrought by war abandoned the loyalty and filial piety ethic, started to feel that *giri* and *ninjō* were old-fashioned, and began to live without fear of reproach for "forgetting their obligations," they at last came to realize that the deepest desire impelling them in practice was *amae* and that this *amae* was, moreover, badly hurt. At the same time, one suspects, they began to perceive as though for the first time that *amae* belonged, originally, to the infant. Of course, to say that the *amae* mentality is infantile does not necessarily mean that it is without value. One need only refer to Japanese history for proof that, far from being valueless, it has provided a driving force behind a large number of cultural values. Nor are these cultural values something of the past, but live in the Japanese of the present day. Yet I doubt if the Japanese of the future will be able to boast without misgivings of the purity of the Japanese spirit. The aim from now on, surely, must be to overcome *amae*. Nor will it do simply to return to the Zen world of identity between subject and object; rather, it will be necessary to transcend *amae* by discovering the subject and object: to discover, in other words, the other person.

Amae and freedom

The Japanese word *jiyū*, usually used to translate the English word "freedom" and other Western words of similar meaning, is of Chinese origin, but seems to have been used in Japan from an early date. What is interesting for us here is that the meaning in which it was traditionally used—as suggested by the combination *jiyū-kimama* ("fancy free")—seems to have a close connection with the desire for *amae*. "Freedom" in Japan, in other words, has traditionally meant the freedom to *amaeru*, that is, to behave as one pleases, without considering others. Never was it freedom from *amae*. Wilfulness, of course, is not considered to be a good thing, and in the same way the word *jiyū*, judging from examples found in old Chinese and Japanese documents, often has, as Tsuda Sōkichi has pointed out,[56] overtones that are to a certain degree critical. In this it is the exact opposite of "freedom" or "liberty," for which *jiyū* served as the translation following the Meiji Restoration but which in the West signify respect for the human being and contain no trace of criticism. For this reason the word *jiyū* has come in recent years to partake of both its good, Western sense and its bad, Japanese sense, with a resulting extreme ambiguity in the concept itself. In what follows I should like to examine this question in somewhat more detail.

First, something should be said concerning the idea of freedom in the West. Historically speaking, it seems to have begun with the distinction between freeman and slave in ancient Greece. Freedom, in other words, meant an absence of the enforced obedience to another implied in the state of slavery; it is precisely because of this that in the West freedom became tied up with ideas such as the rights and dignity of man, and came to be seen as something good and desirable. Parallel with this, the Western-style idea of freedom also serves as a basis for asserting the precedence of the individual over the group, in which respect again it affords a marked contrast with the Japanese idea of *jiyū*. If, as I have done above, one interprets *jiyū* as the right to do what one pleases (*wagamama*), there is undoubtedly, here too, a certain desire on the part of the individual—out of dislike, for example, of interference by the group—to be able to behave just as he pleases. Here, though, it is because the group will not fall in with the individual's wishes that the desire for freedom arises, in which respect the individual remains fundamentally unable to transcend the group. In other words, Japanese-style idea of *jiyū* cannot serve as grounds for asserting the superiority of the individual over the group. There is nothing surprising in this when one considers that originally Japanese-style *jiyū* has its origins in *amae*, since *amae* requires the presence of others: it may make the individual dependent on the group, but it will never allow him to be independent of it in the true sense. Contrary to this, there is the fact that in the West with its emphasis on the freedom of the individual, people have always looked down on the type of emotional dependency that corresponds to *amae*. Generally speaking, there is not even any convenient term to convey this type of emotion in the way that *amae* does.

All kinds of arguments could probably be adduced to show that the Western concept of freedom depends on a rejection of *amae*, but I would like here to quote the following passage attributed to the Renaissance Scholar Juan Luis Vives (1492–1540): "Passive love, that is, the tendency to be the recipient of love, produces gratitude; and gratitude is always mixed with shame. Shame would naturally interfere with the sense of gratitude." When I came across this quotation in Zilboorg's history of psychology[57] I was immediately reminded of the Japanese *sumanai*. I have already explained this use of *sumanai*, in reply to some mark of good will, as an apology for a burden imposed on the other; no Japanese will find anything odd or peculiar in this. Sometimes, even, *sumanai* is replaced by *kyōshuku desu* or *itamiirimasu*, (both meaning something like "I am overcome" or "I am awe-stricken") which if anything are considered superior as expressions of gratitude. People in the West, however, as the Vives quotation suggests, seem to feel that thanks carry with them shame, which in turn hinders the feeling of gratitude. In the attempt to wipe out the sense of shame the Westerner, one might suspect, has striven for long years not to feel excessive gratitude, and thus passive love. There is no doubt, of course, that this has fortified the individual's sense of freedom. It is very interesting in this connection that the proverb "The Lord helps those who help themselves" was not originally derived from Judaism or Christianity but first appeared in George Herbert's *Outlandish Proverbs* published in 1640.[58] This proverb, which is also quoted in Algernon Sidney's *Discourses Concerning Government*,[59] signifies that in a world where all men are each other's enemies the only safe course is self-reliance and self-defense. The aim of the proverb, in other words, is to act as a warning against reliance on god or man, and is completely opposite in spirit from the Japanese proverb *tabi wa michizure, yo wa nasake* (on a journey, a companion; in life, compassion). This trend, which seems to have grown increasingly marked in the West from Renaissance times on into modern times, happens to coincide with the increasing consciousness of the liberty of the individual.

Thus the spirit of *amae* and freedom of the individual would seem to be contradictory with each other. If this is true, then contact with Western-style freedom must have been a considerable shock for the Japanese following the Meiji Restoration. Had they at that point been able really to appreciate individual freedom, they might have been able to rise above the conflict of *giri* and *ninjō* that had always held them in toil, but this was not to be achieved so easily. Most of them were fated to suffer new conflicts through not being able to attain the desired freedom. Ironically, the "Western-style" freedom they thought they were seeking was probably, in fact, a Japanese-style freedom. The trouble stems from the confusion concerning the meaning of *jiyū*; it has even been suggested that *jiyū* is a mistranslation of freedom, but whatever the case since Meiji times the Japanese have been obsessed by a conflict concerning freedom, something clearly illustrated in modern Japanese literature.

To illustrate this, I shall use an episode[60] from *Botchan* by Natsume Sōseki, in whose works I have long been interested. The hero Botchan, unlike the people about him, who live in a state of emotional interdependence, stoutly insists on his own freedom without the need for shame or deference to others. In his outward behavior, he is typical of a man who has breathed the new "free" atmosphere of Meiji times. Yet even he, once he is led astray by the slander of Redshirt, promptly becomes suspicious of Yamaarashi, whom he had trusted at first, and feels obliged to insist on repaying one-and-a-half sen, the cost of an ice to which the latter once treated him. The mentality he shows here seems to me to demonstrate just how fragile was his sense of freedom; let us see first, though, what Botchan himself has to say:

"Yamaarashi was the first to buy me an ice after my arrival here. It was a slight to my pride to accept even an ice from a two-faced type like him. I had only had one glass, so Yama-arashi couldn't have paid more than 1.5 sen. But even at one sen or half a sen to have accepted a favor from a swindler leaves a lifelong unpleasantness. When I go to school tomorrow, I will return the 1.5 sen. I once borrowed three yen from Kiyo. Five years have gone by but still I haven't returned it. Not that I can't, I just don't. Kiyo is not in any way relying on me to pay it back immediately. And me—I've no intention of feeling an obligation to return it immediately, as though she were a stranger. It would be as though I didn't take her kindness at its face value—like finding fault with the goodness of her heart. Not to return it doesn't mean I don't think she matters; it's because I consider she's a part of myself. Kiyo and Yama-arashi just can't be compared of course, but to accept a favor from someone who's not one of your own people and to do nothing about returning it is doing him a favor, because it means you're treating him like somebody who matters to you. If you pay your own share, the matter ends there, but to have a feeling of gratitude inside for a favor done you—that's the kind of repayment no money can buy. I may be a person of no importance, but I'm an independent human being. For an independent human being to bow his head to someone—why, that's the kind of thanks no amount of money could buy."

The noteworthy thing here is the way that Botchan—having shown in saying "I may be a person of no importance but I'm an independent human being" that he has awoken to the freedom of the individual—is earnestly grappling with the significance of the act of gratitude. Gratitude means "bowing one's head" to someone, but that does not matter where the other person is someone one can respect. He also sees gratitude as an "act of kindness" to the other person, and asserts that it is "the kind of repayment that no amount of money could buy." This might be seen as a truly profound discussion of the act of gratitude if it were not for an oddly pompous note in what Botchan says. He discusses the question of showing gratitude to another person, yet manages to convey an overbearing sense that the other person ought to be grateful for his gratitude. Surely one may detect here a case where the sense of shame accompanying gratitude of which Vives spoke has turned into its opposite. If it were not so, how could Botchan, once he had lost faith in Yamaarashi, have paid him back for a trifling favor, for all the world as though this were an act of retaliation?

I suspect that there are a large number of Japanese who, though they would not perhaps behave in such an extreme fashion, would be driven into a state of mind similar to Botchan's in a similar situation. When someone shows them good will, they are overawed. Even when they may not seem so ostensibly, they feel overwhelmed in their inner hearts. This does not matter so long as the relationship with the other is a good one, but should a crack develop in it, the feeling suddenly becomes an intolerable burden. Unless the individual does something, he feels that his freedom (*jiyū*) will be encroached upon, and feels obliged to repay the debt in some way or other. Once awakened to awareness of individual freedom in this way, the Japanese is, precisely for that reason, forced to become more sensitive than someone who has not awoken to it. The freedom of the individual for the Japanese is something, one might say, that has to be accorded "fragile, with care" treatment.

On the other hand, people in the West, for whom individual freedom is part of their very being, do not normally show the over-sensitive reaction of the Japanese. Even among Westerners, of course, one encounters the occasional person peculiarly prone to *amae*, and others, possibly influenced by long contact with Japanese, who acquire a progressively overawed manner in expressing gratitude. Nevertheless, the Westerner's expression of thanks is generally speaking, brief and to the point, with no unpleasant aftermath. If he says "thank you," that "finishes" it; there is none of the Japanese's lingering sense that—as the word *sumanai* literally signifies—things "are not finished."

Why should this be? Why should individual freedom be such an essential and indestructible part of the Westerner's fiber? Can it be because the history of the West, compared with that of Japan, has seen so many violent political upheavals that the individual has come to feel the need to protect himself in everything? I cannot believe that this is enough to explain things. I cannot help feeling that in the West there was some special spiritual legacy that linked together the act of expressing gratitude and the freedom of the individual human being. The spiritual heritage that obviously comes to mind here is Christianity. To discuss Christianity here may seem rather out of place, but since the consideration of *amae* and freedom has brought us so naturally to this point, I take the opportunity to put forward a few of my own views on the subject.

Before beginning, however, I should like to go back to *Botchan* for a moment and try to explain the kind of case where a Japanese feels gratitude without any accompanying sense of awe. As we have already seen, in Botchan's view of things to feel a sense of gratitude and obligation towards someone who is outside one's own personal circle means that "an independent human being" has to bow his head. It is inevitably accompanied by a certain amount of discomfort, and he contrasts this sharply with his feeling toward the maidservant Kiyo. He is, at that very moment, in debt to her, but he has no intention of paying her back. To assume that she was expecting him to pay her back would be like doubting her sincerity, tantamount to finding fault with her fine feelings. His not repaying the debt was not taking her lightly, it was sign that he felt she was on his own side.

Is Botchan, then, grateful for her kindness or not? One could hardly assert that he is not. And yet, one has the feeling that never once has he actually thanked her explicitly. Since he considered her as one of his own people, to do so would have been too coldly formal. Yet this also implies that he himself is not, in fact, independent of her as a human being. It is precisely because the two are part of one whole that it is impossible that one of them should bow his head in thanks to the other. Any Japanese, I suspect, could understand this reasoning. When the Japanese feel grateful, they either express it with a great show of being awestricken or they refrain from saying anything at all. In particular, the more intimate the relationship the fewer the expressions of gratitude; between husband and wife or parent and child words of thanks are normally almost unknown. I am not sure whether this was always so or whether it has become particularly true in recent years, and there may be certain differences according to class or level of society. Either way, it is not incorrect to say that where gratitude is not expressed the two sides, just as in the case of Botchan and Kiyo, are not independent of each other.

Now the habit of the Japanese of feeling as a burden the kindness of *tanin* towards whom they feel some constraint yet accepting without so much as a "thank you" the kindness of their private circle with whom they feel at one is so completely natural to the Japanese themselves that they may even find it odd that there could be any other way of feeling at all. In such a world, there is no freedom and independence of the individual in the strict sense of the word. What appears to be freedom and independence of the individual is no more than an illusion. Yet what if there were some being, essentially superior to mankind, that would bestow freedom on the individual as a gift? In that case, however much gratitude one felt, there would surely be no need to feel that one's freedom had been infringed.

It is precisely here, I suspect, that the central message of Christianity lies. On this score Paul, the first Christian thinker, said: "Christ set us free, to be free men. Stand firm, then, and refuse to be tied to the yoke of slavery again."[61] He expanded and deepened the concepts of freeman and slave that had originated in social discrimination, and used them to expound the two possibilities open to man—freedom through Christ and the slavery of sin. If one reads his epistles one has a vivid impression of what freedom meant to him in his life. He was not troubled in the slightest either by the Judaic tradition in which he had been originally brought up or by pagan customs. The possibility of man's being free, as is signified by the expression "freedom in Christ" arose, of course, because Christ himself was completely free. One might say that it was because he was too free that he was killed, and the faithful believe, moreover, that he even won freedom over death itself.

This idea of freedom in Christ was inherited by St. Augustine and by Luther in turn, but in Luther's case in emphasizing the freedom he also, one suspects, transformed it. As Luther himself saw things, the freedom of which he spoke was—as is clear from his celebrated pamphlet "*On the Freedom of a Christian*"[62]— from first to last freedom because of Christ, yet his rebellion against the political control of the Church of Rome led in time to an increasing emphasis on freedom in the sense of individual freedom in the face of political oppression. In Luther, one might say, the awareness of the freeman in the political sense that first developed in ancient Greece re-emerged under the name of freedom in Christ.

Luther himself of course had no such idea; he even, oddly enough, denied free will in man. He was contradictory in his actual behavior too, in that he opposed the Church of Rome in the name of divine justice, yet used violence to suppress the peasants when they opposed him. Unfortunately, this same contradiction was to be inherited from Luther and persist throughout pre-modern times and up to the present.

The strong awareness of ideas of individual or political freedom that began to make itself felt in the West around the beginning of the modern period was probably related to the gradual breakup, for a variety of causes, of the feudal political setup of the middle ages. Many other champions of political freedom apart from Luther appeared in rapid succession—so many that Luther himself is sometimes struck from the list as having been, if anything, a medieval man in his outlook. Nevertheless, even in cases other than Luther the new free European still wore in some form or other a mantle of Christianity that distinguished him from the freeman of ancient Greece. This Christian mantle became progressively more threadbare as time went on, till finally there occurred a transformation to the secular individualism and liberalism of modern times, yet these still—as the "ism" itself implies—retained a considerable ideological, and thus religious aura. To put it differently, whereas the freeman of ancient Greece knew that he was free without thinking about it, the modern European believed in individual freedom as an article of faith. Individualism and liberalism as a kind of secular religion have persisted to this day, sometimes in conflict with, sometimes in a subtle blend with orthodox Christianity. Today, partly because powerful totalitarian regimes have begun to suppress both the individual's political freedom and Christianity, the forces representing the two latter tend to collaborate with each other, a situation which makes it still more difficult to answer the question of what is freedom.

This—perhaps rather rash—digression outside my own field has been made in order to pose the following question: is the freedom of the individual, that magnificent article of faith for the modern Western world, really to be believed in, or is it merely an illusion cherished by one section of the population of the West? Western man in the early twentieth century, even after the experience of World War I, still harbored a great pride in the idea of freedom that was his spiritual legacy. That fine historian and sociologist Troeltsch, for example, wrote as follows: "The idea of Personality, which, in the form of Freedom, determines everything in the morality of conscience, and, in the form of Object, everything in the ethic of values—this idea is, after all, a Western belief, unknown in our sense to the Far East, and preeminently and peculiarly the destiny of us Europeans."[63] It is true that even today men in the West still behave on the assumption that the individual is free, so that there is considerable difference between their behavior and that of the Japanese who lack their faith. But there are signs that that faith has recently begun to deteriorate into an empty shell.

In short, modern Western man is gradually being troubled by the suspicion that freedom may have been only an empty slogan. The incisive analyses of Marx, who insisted that capitalism inevitably alienated the human being; Nietzsche, who proclaimed that Christianity was the morality of slaves; and the psychoanalysis of Freud, who emphasized the control of the spiritual life by the unconscious, all helped to open the eyes of modern Western man on this point. As a result, his faith in freedom has been cruelly broken. Admittedly, there are some thinkers such as Sartre who cling to human freedom as the only absolute in a society whose superstructure is in process of collapse. Yet where does this type of freedom lead? Ultimately, it can only mean—if not the simple gratification of individual desires—solidarity with others through participation, in which case the Western idea of freedom becomes ultimately something not so different from the Japanese.

In short, the translation of freedom as *jiyū*, though it would seem to have been inappropriate, was not so, since freedom never existed outside the world of faith. Though Marx, Nietzsche, and Freud destroyed the faith in freedom of the modern Western man, no new freedom was to be born in its place. The West as we see it today is caught in a morass of despair and nihilism. It is useful to remember here that the Japanese experience long ago taught the psychological impossibility of freedom. For the Japanese, freedom in practice existed only in death, which was why praise of death and incitements towards death could occur so often. This occurred, of course, because the Japanese were living according to the *amae* psychology, but it is equally true that all the attempts of modern Western man to deny or to sidestep *amae* have not been enough to transcend it, much less to conquer the lure of death. Both in the religious and secular fields, the faiths that have sustained the West may have been deceptions, a kind of opiate, and realization of this may have driven Western men at times to their deaths. If that is so, then they too, I would conclude, have been prey to a hidden *amae*.

The concept of *ki*

The word *ki* originally came from Chinese, so that the concept of *ki* in that language undoubtedly had an influence on the use of the word in Japanese, but here I am concerned with the concept of *ki* mainly as it can be known through idioms of

95

Japanese origin, since the term *ki* appears in a large number of Japanese expressions dealing with emotion, temperament, and behavior and seems to have acquired, as a concept, a different flavor from that which it had in Chinese. To glance at the entries under *ki* in any dictionary of the Japanese language is to find a very large number of special idioms using the term. Ideas corresponding to the English adjectives guilty, capricious, queer, crazy, irritable, narrow-minded, short-tempered, depressed, apprehensive, reluctant, genial, impatient, sensible, generous, frank smart—to name only a few—can all be expressed by idioms in which *ki* is the key word.

Such examples would suggest that *ki* is used chiefly in expressions relating to the emotional life, but there are some that can be taken as referring to the workings of the judgement, the consciousness, or the will. Again, in cases such as *ki ga togameru*, the *ki* seems to mean something like "conscience," which though of course related to emotion is a rather special case. Words such as *risei* (reason), *kanjō* (emotion), *ishiki* (consciousness), *ishi* (will), *ryōshin* (conscience) and so on are originally translations of words from European languages, and it is a peculiarity of the concept of *ki* in the Japanese language that it is an all-purpose term which covers all these cases. In what follows, therefore, I intend to consider the meaning of *ki* in comparison not with the concepts of European languages but with other terms in Japanese relating to the functions of the mind. Terms apart from *ki* that at once come to mind as referring to such functions are *atama* (head), *kokoro* (heart), *hara* (belly), and *kao* (face).

Where *atama* is concerned, little explanation is required. "Head" obviously refers to the power to think or the act of thinking, though sometimes, as in the expressions *atama ga sagaru* (to admit to inferiority, to defer to) or *atama ga takai* (arrogant) it refers to one's attitude in relations with others. These two latter cases may seem to be simple literal descriptions of human behavior, but the first indicates respect for the other's "head" and the second a corresponding lack of respect. Of course, it happens sometimes that the head is, literally, drooped low or held high.

Kokoro means the power to feel emotion towards things or the actual emotion which is felt. Since the meaning here is very close to that of *ki*, there are various cases of parallel expressions, one using *ki* and the other *kokoro*, that have almost identical meanings. Compared with *ki*, however, *kokoro* is a broader, and hence a richer concept. One may speak of a *kokoro* being deep (*fukai*) or shallow (*asai*), or of the "inner recesses" of the *kokoro*, but there are no corresponding expressions for *ki*. This, I feel, automatically gives some gauge of the concept of *ki*; however, I will leave this point for later consideration and turn first to the meaning of *hara* (belly). Just as the belly is that part of the body where things gather or pile up, so the same word when used as a metaphor for spiritual things seems to refer to the self as an accumulation, or compendium of the individual's experience, and thus to something which is not readily shown or apparent to others. *Kao*, "face," is similar to the original Latin *persona*, which meant mask—a surface that one showed to others and hence a front that could be deceptive—whereas in the West the word "person" came to have a far more profound significance.

To turn back finally to *ki*, then, the sense is, as we have seen, close to that of *kokoro*, but in the stricter sense it is different, and it is different also, of course, from the meanings of *atama* and *hara*. Judging from the ways in which it is used, *ki* is perhaps most accurately defined as the movement of the spirit from moment to moment. In other words, where *atama*, *kokoro*, and *hara* all indicate the site where the various workings of the spirit take place, and the things that lie in the background of the phenomenon, *ki* indicates the working of the phenomenon as such. This is well illustrated, I believe, by the expression *ki wa kokoro* (*ki* is *kokoro*), since this means that though something one does may seem trivial, it is nevertheless a manifestation of one's heart. Normally, although one says "*ki* is *kokoro*," one does not say "*ki* is *atama*" or "*ki* is *hara*," yet if the definition of *ki* just given in correct, it should be possible to get some idea of both *atama* and *hara* via the phenomenon of *ki*. One might say, for example, he *ki ga kiku* (is quick on the uptake), therefore he has a good head; or he *ki ni shinai* (doesn't bother himself about such things) since he *hara ga dekite iru* (has got his own personality). Admittedly, someone may have a good head even without *ki ga kiku*, and *ki ni shinai* does not necessarily mean *hara ga dekite iru*, probably because the workings of the *atama* and the *hara* are more complicated and often cannot be detected as *ki* phenomena. In this sense, perhaps, the expression *ki wa kokoro* has its justification, and it is the workings of the "heart" that are most easily detected via the phenomena of *ki*.

Ki also appears as the subject in descriptions of all kinds of workings of the mind, such as *ki ga shizumu* (*ki* sinks, i.e., to be depressed) and *ki ga muku* (*ki* turns in that direction, i.e. to feel inclined to do something). Taken together they give some clue as to the guiding principles behind these workings.

In other words, although people may differ, the *ki* at work in each of them seems to follow the same principle. Of course, this "same principle" does not mean that different people nesessarily get along well because it may happen that their *ki* do not match. But the very emphasis on the discrepancy in their *ki* suggests that the thing that the *ki* of each is seeking after is the same. In other words, both are, essentially, looking for something that fits in with the self, for which reason, a failure of the two *ki* to match is experienced as something unpleasant.

If, now, one observes not merely cases of *ki* matching or not matching but all other activities of *ki* as well, it is possible to conclude that *ki* is constantly concerned with the pursuit of pleasure. And it is precisely here that the principle of the mental activity lies. It corresponds more or less with Freud's "pleasure principle," but where Freud postulated the reality principle alongside the pleasure principle, in Japan no attention is paid to any principle regulating mental activity apart from the pleasure principle.

This point will become still clearer if one examines the true meaning of the expression *ki-mama* ("just as the *ki* takes one" or something like "fancy-free"), the very existence of which presupposes that *ki* is preoccupied with the pursuit of satisfaction. *Ki-mama* is usually equated with *waga-mama* (headstrong, self-willed, selfish), and the dictionaries bow to this, but strictly speaking there is a subtle shade of difference between the two. *Waga-mama* usually carries an overtone of implied criticism, but this is not necessarily so with *ki-mama*. Again, one says *waga-mama o tōsu* (to push through one's *waga-mama*, i.e. have one's own way), but one does not say *ki-mama o tōsu*. This difference may be related to the fact that whereas *waga-mama* is frequently used in relation to third persons *ki-mama* can be used of oneself as well. To live *ki-mama ni*, as the "fancy takes one," is in one sense an enviable state. In Japanese society, *waga-mama* is not, on principle, permitted, but *ki-mama*, interestingly enough, is not frowned upon so long as it does not become *waga-mama*.

The inference one may perhaps draw from this is as follows. *Amae* is, essentially, a matter of dependence on the object, a desire for the identification of subject and object. Thus *waga-mama*, with its naked *amae*, is an attempt not merely to depend on the other person, but also to dominate him. However, if one regards *amae* as a function of *ki*, it is possible to a certain extent to objectivize it and, to the extent that this is successful, establish one's boundary, thus maintaining a distance between oneself and the other person. One might see the development of the special concept of *ki* within Japanese society, dominated

99

as it is by *amae*, as an outcome of some process such as this.

I should like, finally, to add something concerning the concepts of *ki no yamai* (sickness of the spirit) and *kichigai* (a breakdown of the spirit). *Ki no yamai* is a condition in which something goes wrong with the *ki* because it is obstructed in its pursuit of the pleasurable. To put it in different terms, the functioning of *ki* is normally accompanied by a subjective awareness of freedom, but in the case of *ki no yamai* this awareness is lacking. Next, *kichigai* refers to cases where something has gone wrong with the *ki's* propensity for pleasure as such. In short, the *ki* has become abnormal, or in some cases can be considered to have disappeared altogether. Interestingly enough, *ki no yamai* and *kichigai* correspond, respectively, to the modern terms *shinkeishō* (neurosis) and *seishinbyō* (psychosis), both translations from European languages. Moreover, they reveal the essential nature of spiritual disorder far better than these translated terms, and even than the original European terms. Unfortunately, the trend in Japan today is to shun the terms *ki no yamai* and *kichigai* as unscientific popular expressions. They are replaced nowadays in most cases by *noiroze*, i.e. the German word *Neurose*, though amusingly enough the use of this term exactly parallels that of *ki no yamai* and *kichigai*. What is popularly referred to as *noirozegimi* (a tendency to, a touch of, neurosis) is in fact *ki no yamai* and corresponds to neurosis, while *hommono no noiroze* (real neurosis) means *kichigai* and from a specialist point of view refers in most cases to mental illness more serious than neurosis. This is probably due to the fact that the ideas of *ki no yamai* and *kichigai* are still firmly rooted in the Japanese sensibility. Either way, the Japanese language is very handy not only where these terms for mental illness are concerned but in conveying all gradations of psychopathology in general. I shall go into this in more detail in the next chapter.

4 The pathology of *amae*

The *toraware* mentality

Toraware is a name given by Morita Shōma to the mental process which he believed to be common to the type of patient whose symptoms are referred to in Japan as *shinkeishitsu*, nervousness, a general term applied to patients who complain of various physical symptoms such as headache, palpitations, fatigue, or distension of the stomach yet in whom examination shows no physical abnormality. The same term is sometimes used of patients who apart from such physical symptoms complain strongly of feelings of fear, apprehension or shame. Morita has the following to say concerning how *shinkeishitsu* comes about:

"If the attention is concentrated on a particular sensation, that sensation becomes more acute, and this acuteness of sensation fixes the attention more and more in the same direction; sensation and attention intereact on each other, so that the sensation becomes increasingly great."[64] Morita called this process "mental interreaction" or, using a basic, everyday word, "*toraware*" (preoccupation, obsession), and in advising his patients, it seems, he sometimes actually used the expression "you're *torawareru* (obsessed, preoccupied) with. . . ." And undoubtedly it frequently happened, where the case was not very serious, that the patient who had thought he had something physically wrong with him, or who had some irrational fear, would feel better at the simple realization that it was true.

Morita's achievement in perceiving this element of *toraware* in the nervous patient was considerable, yet the theory of mental interaction that he put forward seems rather inadequate in itself. Simply as a phenomenon, it is true that what appears to be an interaction between attention and sensation is not infrequently to be observed in *shinkeishitsu* patients. However, this is a kind of vicious circle, and as with all vicious circles there has to be some other cause to precipitate it. No doubt Morita noticed this point himself; which is probably why he stated that the reason for this mental interaction was a "hypochondriac disposition." This requires that one define the "hypochondriac disposition," but Morita dismissed it simply as the fear of disease or death common to everybody. That may have disposed of it in theory, but of course simply to explain all this to the patient did not automatically mean disappearance of the fears and a cure of the preoccupation. This, it seems, is why Morita adopted work therapy—as a means of drawing the patient's attention away from the interreaction—at the same time using supervised diary writing and supervised group discussion as a means of bringing home repeatedly to the patient the fact of his *toraware*.

The reason why I have gone into Morita's theory in some detail is that one can see his *toraware* as related to, and a pathological variation of, the *amae* psychology. Morita's theory has for long been highly valued in Japan as a uniquely Japanese theory of *shinkeishitsu*, and as such has been widely reported in other countries. If, now, his *toraware* should prove to be a mental reaction with affinities with *amae*, this would be still more true than ever. I was brought to this view in the course of treating *shinkeishitsu* patients by psychoanalytical methods. They were all excessively sensitive towards other people, and showed enormous restraint and "difficulty" (*kodawari*) even in the relationships developed as part of the treatment, but it was noticeable that as this kind of feeling towards others grew stronger, their symptoms lessened in intensity.

As I have already said, *kigane* (restraint) and *kodawari* (being difficult) have their origins in concealed *amae*; from which, I drew the following conclusion. This kind of patient is in a state of mind where he cannot *amaeru* even if he wants to—which is the breeding-ground of his basic anxiety. Unable to wrap up that anxiety successfully within himself, he lives a constant prey to it, and accordingly connects it up with what is in reality some trivial physical reaction, which gives rise to the state of *toraware*. This theory of mine may be new insofar as it interprets *toraware* in the light of *amae*, but far from conflicting with Morita's theory it would seem to me to deepen it still further, doing no more than illuminate the psychological structure of the hypochondriac disposition postulated by Morita.

As we have seen, Morita's originality lies in the attention he drew to the *toraware* psychology as early as 1900, and his theories of *shinkeishitsu* can justly be called a fine piece of original scholarship, yet even so the human psychology does not vary so very greatly from place to place. Though it may appear different, it invariably rests on common foundations. In particular, the "nervous" reaction that Morita studied is to be found in the West also, and it would be odd indeed if patients there did not show the *toraware* psychology that Morita pointed out. It is merely that in the past no Western scholar noticed it, a fact probably deriving from the existence in the average Westerner of psychological tendencies that tend to obscure it. It is interesting, nevertheless, that in recent years a few scholars have appeared who, independently of Morita's work, have discussed something that corresponds to *toraware*. One of them, G. A. Ladee[65] of Holland, states that the essence of hypochondria is the feeling that one is affected by some pathological change, plus a fascination with that feeling. The

103

English word "fascination" which he uses for this preoccupation is obviously identical with *toraware*. Again, the German scholar Walter Schulte[66] sets forth, as a goal in the treatment of nervous patients, "die Unbefangenheit zu leben," in other words, to live without *toraware*, a goal which he said had not been set forth before in writing. In this way, the *toraware* psychology pointed out by Morita has recently and quite independently been recognized by two scholars in other countries, but neither of them have probed this *toraware* further to discover the *amae* that lies beneath.

Fear of others

The expression *taijin kyōfu* (fear of others, anxiety in dealing with other people), which it seems was first used by the psychiatrists who succeeded to the mantle of Morita, has by now become an indispensable term in Japanese psychiatry. It is almost the only case of a specialist term used in psychiatry that does not smack of translation from some Western language; most other terms have still not settled in as items of Japanese vocabulary, and they are difficult for the layman to grasp. It is an exception, almost certainly, because it came into existence chiefly as a result of observation of Japanese patients. The patients labelled by Morita as showing nervous symptoms included a considerable number who complained of various fears in dealing with others—fear of blushing, fear of meeting the other's gaze, anxiety concerning their own ugliness, anxiety concerning their own body odor, and so on. What is more, even where the patient does not complain explicitly of this kind of difficulty, almost all patients whose case is serious enough to be diagnosed as *shinkeishitsu* have experienced some difficulty in relations with others. A proof of this, already mentioned, is that this type of patient becomes strongly aware of feelings of restraint (*kigane*) and difficulty (*kodawari*) in the course of treatment. The prominence among *shinkeishitsu* patients in Japan of this kind of anxiety in relations with others, whether in the broad or the narrow sense, is attributed by scholars of the Morita school to historical and social circumstances affecting the Japanese.

Extremely interesting in this connection is the use of the word *hitomishiri*,[67] literally, coming to know people, which is usually translated in the dictionaries simply as "shyness" or "bashfulness." In practice, it is normally applied to infants, though occasionally it is used of young adults also. Let us examine a few typical examples of its use.

Kono ko wa mō hitomishiri suru (this child already shows *hitomishiri*) is used of babes-in-arms, and refers to the way a baby comes to distinguish its mother from other people, objecting when held by others but calming down immediately it is taken into its mother's arms. This is identical with the phenomenon which the psychoanalyst R. Spitz called "eight-month anxiety" or "stranger anxiety,"[68] and it is significant that a phenomenon to which in the West attention was first drawn by a scholar should have been noted, in the term *hitomishiri*, by mothers in Japan—and not especially educated mothers at that—since olden times. In the sentence just quoted, *hitomishiri* is regarded as an achievement, as an indicator of the child's mental development, but there are other times when, for example, a mother may say "this child's *hitomishiri* is far too strong." In the latter case, it indicates that although the child is no longer an infant at the breast it makes no move to leave its mother and, in particular, tends to shy away from strangers. The word *hitomishiri* is sometimes used in a similar sense of adults, when it becomes synonymous with "self-consciousness" in the sense of shyness or embarrassment. One may say, for example, "I tend to *hitomishiri*, so I don't like visiting strangers."

The word *hitomishiri*, thus, is rich in overtones; not only does it refer to the time when the infant first begins to look at people, but its use extends to the development of the personality and on through the adult period, where it is used to describe the phenomenon of an adult avoiding strangers in the same way as a child that has just acquired the ability to distinguish between people. The latter case, which can be regarded as a kind of late development, is fairly commonly found among the Japanese and in itself can hardly be described as morbid, though if the tendency is too strong the person concerned naturally suffers. *Shinkeishitsu* patients, who frequently complain of difficulty in dealing with other people, correspond to this case, while those diagnosed as *taijin kyōfu*, with such symptoms as blushing, unable to meet the gaze of others, anxiety about personal appearance, body odor, and so on, can be considered as persons whose personalities have been fashioned by the development of *hitomishiri* to a morbid degree. That account has always been taken of *hitomishiri* in Japan is extremely convenient in considering the origins of difficulty or anxiety in dealing with others. It can also be seen as backing up the claim of the Morita school that this type of difficulty is common in Japan.

Before examining in rather more detail the relationship between *hitomishiri* and a morbid degree of anxiety in dealing with others, let us consider *hitomishiri* in the infant, where it first occurs. The first *hitomishiri*, as we have already seen, happens when the infant recognizes its mother and distinguishes her from others. This development, which occurs because of the child's realization of the necessity of the mother, can also be described as the beginning of the child's *amae* towards her. The infant's *amae* can, in fact, be said to begin simultaneously with *hitomishiri*. This makes it not unreasonable to suppose that *amae* is also at work where phenomena resembling *hitomishiri* occur in the post-infantile period. *Hitomishiri* and *amae*, in other words, are reverse sides of the same coin. In what can be considered normal development, the first experience of *hitomishiri* is followed by the gradual growth of the infant's ego. Then as it develops connections with people other than its mother it is gradually worked into a broader pattern of human relationships. Even here, in Japanese society, the distinction is always maintained between the inner and outer circles, the individual being protected and permitted to *amaeru* within the inner circle. Since *amae* is not immediately possible with persons outside that circle, however, a certain degree of *hitomishiri* is not considered particularly remarkable. A considerable individual variation is of course at work here. For example, where the individual is by birth excessively sensitive, or where the mother's personality or other environmental factors have helped to hinder a good relationship with the mother during the early stages, the individual, it seems, never transcends the experience of *hitomishiri*, which continues into adulthood, bringing corresponding anxiety in dealing with other people.

Even so, the appearance of fear in dealing with others contains factors that cannot be explained solely in terms of the relationship between mother and child in infancy, since it is frequently observed that a similar anxiety occurs in the individual who leaves a familiar community and goes to live in a new and unfamiliar community. Cases in point are where an individual moves from the country to a large town, or leaves school and goes to work in new surroundings.

Not everybody, of course, experiences anxiety in these circumstances, and individual differences, depending on how well the individual has learned his early lessons, naturally come into play. What I am concerned with here, however, is the social factors that lead the predisposed individual to show these symptoms of anxiety in dealing with others. Particularly important here is the fact that in Japan since the Meiji Restoration social relationships have gradually acquired a different nature

107

from the traditional relationships that prevailed earlier. One might, to borrow Tönnies's[69] terminology, label the change as one from *Gemeinschaft*-type to *Gesellschaft*-type relationships. Japanese society is still, of course, to a considerable degree of the *Gemeinschaft*-type, forming a world where, as we saw in chapter one, *amae* is still dominant, yet there are signs that little by little it is changing into a *Gesellschaft*-type society. For this reason, social relationships today no longer allow the individual to *amaeru* so easily as in the past. Or it may be that society has become so complex that it is no longer easy to discover the rules whereby one may *amaeru* with ease. Either way, the result is that persons in whom *hitomishiri* is strong to begin with suffer more and more from frustrated *amae*, which builds up to the point where it gives rise to neurotic anxiety in dealing with others. This is only a guess, of course, but even if not strictly accurate I feel that it cannot be far from the truth. Thus those who found it impossible to adapt to the new circumstances created by the social upheaval following the Meiji Restoration came in time to display a variety of neurotic symptoms, and it was for these people that the Morita therapy provided such an appropriate solution.

What I have just written can also be confirmed in the light of the gradual shift in the value attached to the sense of shame in modern Japan. Specifically, the shyness and embarrassment a man with *hitomishiri* feels towards strangers is itself a form of shame. I suspect, though, that whereas in traditional Japanese society great importance was attached to the sense of shame, a display of shame being viewed with understanding and even with appreciation, in modern times, under the influence of the West, society as a whole has lost the breadth of spirit necessary, so that the feeling of shame has become, if not an actual disadvantage, at least no advantage to the person concerned. It seems possible that the man who feels shame, sensing that the other person is not prepared to accept his feeling with understanding, turns it in upon himself and becomes tense, which gives rise in turn to such anxiety symptoms as blushing and doubts about his own person. This type of social change has greatly accelerated since the end of World War II, which has had its effect on manifestations of anxiety in the presence of others. A recent study of trends in neurosis among young people[70] shows that recently there has been a gradual decrease in symptoms, such as blushing, that obviously arise from the sense of shame, with an increase in the inability to meet the gaze of others and anxiety concerning body odor— symptoms that were seldom found before and immediately after the war. This conclusion, which corresponds with my own clinical impressions, can probably be interpreted—as the author of the study points out—as a change from "a sense of shame towards one's surroundings" to "a sense of fear towards one's surroundings," the basic reason probably being that society, as stated above, is no longer prepared to accept the individual's display of shame.

Ki ga sumanai

The feeling expressed in the words *ki ga sumanai* ("not to be satisfied," as in the sentence "he's never satisfied unless . . .") is one that arises when things fail to go as one has decided they should. For example: *kono shigoto o kyō-jū ni shiagenai to dōmo ki ga sumanai* "I just shan't be happy unless I get this work finished today." This *ki ga sumanai* mentality appears in very marked form in certain pathological conditions.

I have stated that *ki* indicates the movement of the mind from moment to moment, and that *ki* represents a principle of mental activity that is basically pleasure-oriented. I also added that the Japanese use *ki* as a means of surveying objectively their own mental activity, and of securing freedom, or integrity, of the spirit. If one now examines the expression *ki ga sumanai* from this point of view, one can draw some interesting conclusions. The man who feels *ki ga sumanai* is a man who to some extent is conscious of his own mental activity as an integrated whole. He seeks to satisfy what he is aware of as his *ki*, and he can discard everything else. In that sense, he might almost be called an egotist. He may sometimes appear difficult to deal with. But this also means that he is correspondingly reluctant to rely on others. If one now attempts to differentiate between *sumanai* and *ki ga sumanai*, to feel *sumanai* toward another person means that one's *amae* toward him is kept alive, whereas in feeling *ki ga sumanai* one is attaching less importance to others than to one's own *ki*. The person who is liable to feel *ki ga sumanai*—the compulsive type—can be said to have grown out of the infantile type of *amae* and to rank among the more autonomous type of individual in a society such as Japan's that is permeated through and through with *amae*.

This only refers, however, to the "normal" range, where the individual knows that if he acts in a certain way his compulsion will be satisfied; where it cannot be satisfied and the resulting frustration becomes a continual source of suffering, the reaction is morbid. In the normal case, there is correspondence between the self and the *ki*, but in the pathological case there is a split between the two. The cause of this split is probably that the individual, who seems to have outgrown *amae*, has in fact not done so, so that he harbors a suppressed sense of resentment and mortification (*kuyashisa*). There are differences thus in the degree of satisfaction obtained for *ki* depending on whether the case is normal or pathological, but the expression *ki ga sumanai* is appropriate in both cases.

Now the fact that this same everyday word *ki ga sumanai* can be used both of the normal individual and of the individual suffering from a compulsive neurosis would surely suggest that a compulsive trait is pervasive among the Japanese. Such compulsion is not of course exclusive to the Japanese; it exists in some form or other in every nation, and there may well be other peoples with similar personality traits. However, what one may perhaps describe as a Japanese characteristic is their ability to note and sum up in the one phrase *ki ga sumanai* all the different manifestations of the compulsive tendency. They believe that in such cases it is only natural to behave so that the *ki* is satisfied, and actually consider it praiseworthy to do so.

One might say, for example, that the celebrated Japanese "industriousness" is related to this compulsive trait expressed in the phrase *ki ga sumanai*. In Japan, farm, factory, and office workers throw themselves unquestioningly into their work. It is not so much that they are obliged to do so by poverty, but that if they did not do so they would feel *ki ga sumanai*. They give little consideration to the meaning of their work or to what it will achieve for society as a whole, or for themselves, or for their families. Nor do they hesitate to make a certain degree of sacrifice for the sake of their work. From the point of view of the work itself, this may be an ideal thing, and it is undoubtedly difficult to carry through any work properly without a certain degree of such enthusiasm. What is dangerous, however, is that before he realizes it the individual's motive may shift from the work as such to the feeling that unless he does it *ki ga sumanai*. When a particular stage of his work is finished, of course, even he will feel satisfaction and take a break. But since there is always more work waiting, he soon feels *ki ga sumanai* and starts to feel pressed by work again.

This is such an everyday matter for the Japanese that no-body in the past has given it a second thought, but in its more extreme forms the tendency is the same as a compulsive neurosis. Where, for some reason or other, it has become impossible for the individual to carry on his work and to alleviate the feeling of *ki ga sumanai*, it is not uncommon for him to lapse into a pathological melancholy. The man with the nature that feels unsatisfied unless he is working finds it impossible to take time off from work. Nor can he do something solely for the sake of enjoying himself. Even when he does so, in many cases it is from a sense of obligation or to go along with his colleagues, so that amusement loses its proper significance and becomes in itself a kind of work. Sometimes he and his fellows may get drunk, make a lot of noise and generally raise hell, but this probably indicates merely a desire to escape, if only for a short while, from the *ki ga sumanai* feeling.

With the "leisure boom" of the last few years people have begun to extol the virtues of amusement, but one doubts whether the Japanese have really acquired the ability to amuse themselves without worrying. Even in their amusements, they give the air of amusing themselves because it is the thing to do —in other words, they feel *ki ga sumanai* if they do not do so. It is worth noting here that the very word *asobi* (amusing oneself, play) has a rather derogatory ring compared with its equivalents in the languages of the West. The close correspondence here with the Puritanism of the West is interesting; it may be that Puritanism itself has its roots in a psychological syndrome similar to that just outlined.

This failure to accord any positive value to amusement as such is probably due to the depth to which the Japanese are permeated with the feeling of *ki ga sumanai*. Generally speaking, where work is an objective obligation and limited in its scope, it is possible to be released from the obligation and to enjoy a period of freedom. It is possible also to do work not merely because one feels *ki ga sumanai* but to obtain mental pleasure from the work itself. But when the individual is a slave to compulsion there is no respite for the spirit (*ki*), whether he is at work or at play. This may be the reason why the Japanese are generally held abroad to be earnest and stiff, with no sense of humor. It is an extremely paradoxical idea, but it seems possible that the very desire of the Japanese for *amae* leads them

112

to deny it when they find it difficult to satisfy that desire in practice, so that frequently they get stuck in the constricting state of mind represented by *ki ga sumanai*.

Homosexual feelings

The "homosexual feelings" referred to here are not homosexuality in the narrow sense. The word homosexuality usually refers to the experience of sexual attraction and the inclination to sexual union between members of the same sex, but I use "homosexual feelings" here in a broader sense, to refer to cases where the emotional links between members of the same sex take preference over those with the opposite sex. They correspond roughly, therefore, with what is normally termed "friendship," but where friendship usually lays emphasis only on the good will existing between friends, in this case the emphasis is on the fact that the emotional links that form the basis of friendship take precedence over love between the sexes. Nor is the occurrence of these feelings limited exclusively to friends, for they may occur between teacher and pupil, between senior and junior members of some organization, or even between parent and child of the same sex.

It should be emphasized, moreover, that although these homosexual feelings may exist in conjunction with homosexuality in the narrow sense, they do not always necessarily develop into this restricted type of homosexuality; if anything, the possibility in practice is slight. These homosexual feelings, in themselves, fall within the province of the normal, and are experienced by everybody in the course of growing up, though it seems that there are individual, as well as social and cultural differences in the length of the periods during which such feelings are predominant. It is possible, for example, for an individual who is sexually normal and already leading a normal

113

married life to be emotionally still under the dominance of homosexual emotions.

My realization of the importance of homosexual feelings in Japan was related to the cultural shock which I described in chapter one. I was astonished to discover the special emphasis laid in America, unlike traditional Japanese custom, on the ties between the sexes, not only after marriage but before it as well. It is true that in recent years Japan has come increasingly to resemble America in this respect, but the old tendency would still seem to persist in large measure. For example, when one holds a party in America the sexes are almost always paired off in equal numbers, but this is very rare in Japan. The Japanese very frequently travel in groups, beginning with school excursions and continuing into adult life—when the individual often goes on trips with members of the same firm or other organization to which he belongs—but he is not normally accompanied by his family in such cases. In America, one usually takes one's family with one on trips. Even in America, of course, social contact with members of the same sex exists not only before but even after marriage, but in principle the marriage relationship, or the relationship of lovers, always takes precedence. For members of the same sex always to act together, or to show excessive familiarity, is to lay them open immediately to suspicion of homosexuality, and people are particularly sensitive on this score. Japan, on the other hand, is the ideal place for enjoying friendship with members of the same sex openly and unashamedly. The attraction that homosexuals from the West are said to feel for Japanese society is probably due partly to the absence from the outset in Japanese society of any restraints on homosexuality, and partly to its extreme tolerance of expressions of homosexual feelings.

I know no literary work that portrays so accurately the nature of homosexual emotions in Japanese society as Natsume Sōseki's *Kokoro*. From the moment when the young man who appears as the first-person narrator of the story first catches sight, on the beach at Kamakura, of the character whom he is later to call Sensei, he is attracted towards him and feels a strong urge to make his acquaintance. When the other man swims, for example, he too swims in his wake, but since Sensei takes no notice of him he finds no opportunity to get into conversation. One day, however, the ideal chance occurs when Sensei, coming out of the water, is putting on his summer kimono and his spectacles, which were under the kimono, fall to the floor.

He promptly thrusts head and arm beneath the seat, retrieves the spectacles, and hands them back to Sensei. This gives him the chance to strike up an acquaintance. There is an almost embarrassing resemblance here to the wiles and ruses a man uses in order to strike up a friendship with a woman who has taken his fancy. Either way, the scene conveys the same atmosphere of barely suppressed attraction as is engendered in a similar encounter between man and woman.[71]

The author, it seems, was fully aware of what he was doing when he created this scene, since later in the novel, after the hero has acquired the habit of visiting Sensei, the latter asks him why he comes so often, then later informs him that his visits are "for the sake of love." Startled, the hero insists that it has nothing to do with love, but Sensei persists: it is a stage on the way to love. "You came to my place, a man of the same sex," he explains, "as a stage on the way to making love with the other sex."

Besides this, the novel *Kokoro* contains many other depictions of homosexual feelings at work. It becomes clear that during his student days Sensei had more or less forcibly arranged that his friend K should come to live in his own lodgings—the motive here obviously being of a homosexual nature. At the time, he was interested in his landlady's daughter, but, being also fearful of being caught in a trap laid by the mother, was in a disturbed, indecisive frame of mind. Therefore, he overcame the landlady's opposition and by sharing his lodgings with K sought to restore the spiritual stability that had been upset by his relations with the other sex. The effect was only momentary, however; as soon as K struck up a personal friendship with the landlady and her daughter, Sensei was seized with jealousy. This jealousy was probably due in part to the feeling that the women's love had been stolen from him by K, but was still more due, it seems, to resentment at the interest K showed in the women in preference to himself. He had believed that K's ascetically inclined idealism would keep him out of all entanglements with the opposite sex, and had offered K his passionate friendship on those grounds. This friendship was dealt a severe blow by K's confession to him of his love for the daughter. On the one hand, he reproached K with the identical words that K had earlier used toward him: "A man with no desire to raise himself spiritually is a fool"; and on the other he took his revenge by beating K to the mark and making an agreement with the landlady that he himself would marry her daughter. Immediately he had done so, he felt an acute sense of guilt (*sumanai*) towards K, but a few days later, before he had had a chance to apologize, K committed suicide, and the shock left Sensei prey to a feeling of utter desolation.

Ever since then Sensei has been haunted by K's ghost, till finally he follows K into death by himself committing suicide; yet even at this stage he says not a word to his wife of his profound relationship with K. What clearer exposition of homosexual emotions could one have than this?

My account of *Kokoro* has been rather long, but I would like to make one further point: that the novel does not merely give an accurate account of the precedence given to homosexual feelings in Japanese society, but also presents a criticism of that state of affairs, since the fates of Sensei and K are the most eloquent testimony to the fact that exclusive concentration on male friendship can frequently drive those concerned to destruction. One even suspects that when Sensei remarks cryptically to the hero: "Anyway, love is a sin, d'you know? And it's divine, too." he is thinking not so much of the affair with the landlady's daughter as of his relationship with K. This is backed up by his observation, made immediately afterwards, that the hero's feelings towards himself are suspect.

It would be going too far, of course, to assume that when Sensei talks of love he is referring only to homosexual relationships. One may take the statement that "love is a sin" at its face value, as indicating that love leads to sin, and it makes perfectly good sense as a warning against getting entangled with women. Yet one cannot help feeling that this interpretation is too superficial, and that the author was in fact hinting at something else, for the relationship that the novel is really passing judgment on is Sensei's attitude towards K, which is what in practice spoiled his love relationships with women. Either way, it was his own experience in the past, when his own partiality for K led him, conversely, to take revenge on K, that leads the Sensei to reject the partiality that the hero shows for himself. "You shouldn't," he says on one occasion, "place too much reliance on me. You'll only regret it later, and then you'll take some cruel revenge for the way you've been deceived." He adds: "The memory of having kneeled before someone makes one want to trample him underfoot at a later date. I prefer to forego the reverence of today and avoid the insults to come. I'd rather put up with being lonely now than have to put up with being still more lonely in the future. We live in an age of freedom, independence, and the self, and I imagine this loneliness is the price we have to pay for it."

The speech by Sensei just quoted is remarkably profound in its implications, but in order to understand it properly it is necessary first to make clear just what he is so bitterly reproaching. What has gone before would naturally suggest that the answer is "homosexual feelings," which raises the question of what, ultimately, this means. Is it merely feeling directed at members of the same sex? That is obviously no explanation. There is obviously nothing reprehensible in an emotion simply because it is directed at the same sex. If, now, one goes back to the definition given at the beginning of this section and defines feelings as homosexual in cases where they take precedence, over relations with the opposite sex, the outlines become rather more clearly defined, though still I do not feel that this has got at their essential nature.

Of course, one can get some general clue as to what is at stake from the example just quoted from *Kokoro*, but one might feel some perplexity if asked to express the *Gestalt* in words. I believe, though, that one can throw more light on this point by saying that the essence of these homosexual emotions is *amae*. I hasten to add that *amae* occurs, of course, between opposite sexes and is in no way confined to the case of homosexual emotions. In Japan in particular, *amae* has traditionally been considered to be an emotion experienced between the sexes. *Amae*, generally speaking, is an inseparable concomitant of love (*koi*), and love, as is stated in Plato's *Symposium*, is the same whether the object is of the opposite or the same sex. Even so, I still believe it correct to say that the essence of homosexual feelings is *amae*. Leaving the psychological reasons for believing this until later, I would first point out that to adopt this interpretation makes much clearer what it is that is being criticized in *Kokoro*. This may come as something of a surprise to the Japanese reader insofar as *amae*—whether the *amae* of a child toward its parent, of a student toward his teacher, of a company employee toward his superiors, or of a junior toward his senior—is considered utterly natural in Japanese society. *Amae*, he might say, is surely something essentially innocent, something indispensable in cementing human relationships. Indeed,

118

viewed in this light *amae* might seem more worthy of praise than criticism. Surely, it might be argued, it is the source of those finest flowerings of human contact—friendship, the master-pupil relationship, probably even love itself. The moving quality of the almost erotic relationship between Yoshitsune and Benkei portrayed in Kabuki surely derives from its suggestion of a profound converse of spirits transcending the simple master-servant relationship.

All this is no doubt true. In *Kokoro*, Sensei says, "Love is a sin. . . . And it's divine, too." And one might say that *amae*, too, is holy and innocent. The point here, though, is that *amae* can at the same time become something evil. Obviously, friendship, the master-pupil relationship, and love are not in themselves evil; Sensei's friendship for K also included sympathy and respect, which are unquestionably admirable things in themselves. Then what was it that poisoned the friendship? The answer, surely, is Sensei's *amae* towards K. It was because of *amae* that when Sensei felt he had been neglected by K he took his revenge. The partiality for Sensei shown by the hero of the novel undoubtedly contains a serious desire to learn, a desire that has nothing to do with *amae*. This is an admirable thing—and it is because of it, probably, that Sensei is able in the end to reveal to the hero the wretched truth about himself. Yet at the same time he cannot tolerate the hero's *amae*; for he knows from his own experience how easily this *amae* can turn to hatred. His one hope is that by learning the truth about him, the hero might awaken from his own *amae* and achieve the birth of a new self.

The danger that lurks in *amae* is partly due to the instability of *amae* as such, but it also seems to be due in part to the age in which we live, an age "full of freedom and independence and self." I will leave this point till the last, however, and try now to give an account, with references to Freud's theories on homosexuality, of the justification for stating as I did that the essence of homosexual feelings is *amae*. First, it is widely held that one of the main causes of homosexuality is as follows: for some reason or other the boy is particularly close to his mother during early childhood, with the result that when he reaches the age at which he should begin taking an interest in the other sex he finds it impossible to sever this connection with his mother. He identifies with his mother—he becomes his mother, as it were—and thus comes to love objects that are similar to himself. If homosexuality is in many cases an outcome of closeness to the mother, may it not be possible to see it as an expression of *amae*? It is, indeed, a clinically observed fact that homosexuals show toward each other a degree of *amae* that they would normally be reluctant to show before others. Another interesting thing in the Freudian theory is its statement that homosexual feelings play a hidden pathological role in both neurosis and psychosis. Homosexual feelings, in fact, are a vital concept in Freudian theory as a whole. However, "homosexual feelings" alone is, as we have seen, far too vague a term. It is too much to expect that it should be generally accepted as a concept without elaboration. Closer examination, in order to get at its real essence, was needed, but Freud failed to do so, one reason, I believe, being that he was unfamiliar with the extremely handy concept of *amae*.

Now Freud's theory of homosexual feelings as playing an important role in neurosis and psychosis and Sōseki's ideas as expounded in *Kokoro* seem to be complementary with each other, in so far as Sōseki says that homosexual feelings are unable to cure man's basic loneliness and only make him unhappy. If one replaces the word homosexuality with the word *amae* in both Freud's case and Sōseki's case, their ideas might perhaps be summed up as follows. The frustration or conflicts arising from *amae* bring about all kinds of psychological difficulties. Even where it is satisfied through love, friendship, or the affection between master and pupil, it allows no peace of mind. The satisfaction is temporary and invariably ends in disillusionment. For in a modern age of "freedom, independence, and self," the sense of solidarity with others that comes from *amae* is ultimately no more than a mirage. Both men state that if we do not wish to suffer from disillusionment, we must be resigned to putting up with the truth about ourselves and with the loneliness of isolation.

Kuyamu and *kuyashii*

Two more highly significant words in the Japanese language are the verb *kuyamu*, which means to regret in the sense of "to regret something that has happened over which one has no control, or about which it is too late to do anything," and the adjective *kuyashii*, which means something like "annoying," "vexatious," or "mortifying." They stem from the same root, and their meanings have much in common, since *kuyamu* means to feel that something is *kuyashii*, the "regret" of the former being tinged with the idea of "if only I'd known in time . . ." *Kuyamu*, apparently, is a variation of another verb, *kuiru*, which means to regret or repent of; there is a subtle yet important distinction in the use of the two verbs, since *kuiru* expresses regret over something for which one was responsible oneself, whereas *kuyamu* is an expression of regret at having permitted a cause for regret to remain. In other words, in the case of *kuyamu* simple regret is not enough: one must harp on the feeling of "if only I hadn't . . ." indefinitely in one's own mind. Or one might define *kuyamu* as regret for allowing oneself to fall into a situation where one was obliged to feel regret. *Kuyamu*, in short, represents a far more involved and complex state of mind than *kuiru*. And it seems to me extremely interesting that Japanese should have a simple everyday word to express such a complex state of mind.

121

In mourning the death of another, the Japanese customarily express their regrets to the family of the deceased with the phrase *okuyami mōshiagemasu* (may I express my *kuyami*). For long I failed to see why this should be considered an expression of sympathy with the bereaved, perhaps because it was a long time before I myself had the experience of losing any close relative. When I had that experience, however, I at last came to understand the meaning of the conventional phrase. In short, when I lost someone close to me I felt an intolerable sense of regret. If only, I told myself, I had done this or that. . . . And though I knew that none of my regrets could reverse what had happened, yet still for some time I could not make myself cease regretting. I experienced a new sense of guilt towards the deceased, and at the same time I felt regret at having to feel that guilt. At that time, I realized for the first time that the phrase *okuyami mōshiagemasu* was, in fact, an expression of deep sympathy. Thinking of the deceased, the bereaved family almost certainly feels all kinds of regrets at things done or left undone. The person who comes to express his condolences almost certainly himself feels, if he was close to the deceased during his lifetime, a certain sense of regret, even if not so strong as that of the family. To evoke that regret would seem to be the ideal way of expressing shared feeling with the bereaved.

When one loses someone close to one, one feels not merely the sadness of the loss but also a frequent sense of regret at things done or left undone. And it is for this reason, it seems, that the custom arose, both in the East and in the West, of going into mourning for the dead. It was originally not merely a superficial courtesy towards the deceased, but an established means of assuaging the mental suffering occasioned by the death of someone near and dear. Now, the cause of the mental depression in such a case is clearly defined, but there are other cases where such depression occurs without a clearly established cause. The most typical case is the mental state that used to be

122

called melancholia and is now called, simply, depression. In such cases, the basic cause of the state is not immediately apparent. Despite this, the person concerned remains sunk in a gloomy sense of loss, and is troubled by various regrets over the past. In this respect, the state and the suffering occasioned by the loss of a loved one are very similar, and Freud[72], very logically, tried to throw light on the psychological mechanism of the former by reference to the latter. One wonders how it happened that not one psychologist before Freud should have given this resemblance any consideration.

Now, what I myself find interesting is that Freud did not notice that the sadness occasioned by losing a loved one and depression share in common the *kuyami* mentality. Admittedly, this statement is liable to invite misunderstanding unless one explains it in a little more detail. Since Freud does discuss the excessive feelings of self-reproach that play such a conspicuous part in depression, he might seem to have dealt with the *kuyami* mentality. The question, however, is the nature of the feelings of self-reproach in this case; Freud seems to have had the greatest difficulty in making this point clear, but if he had known the concept expressed by the Japanese term *kuyami* he would almost certainly have found the solution to the problem easier; for the characteristic of the self-reproach found in depression lies in the fact that it is *kuyami*, and not *kui*. Moreover, since the *kuyami* mentality is closely related to that expressed in the adjective *kuyashii* it very conveniently suggests the aggression which, as Freud pointed out, lies concealed in depression.

Of course, as stated at the beginning of this section, *kuyami* and *kuyashisa* derive originally from the same root and their meanings are almost identical, yet the way in which they are used is rather different. Where *kuyami* is entirely introverted, the feeling of *kuyashii*—as in the expression *makete kuyashii* ("how mortifying to have lost," if not colloquial, seems the closest approximation in English)—is to some extent aware of the out-

123

side world. In *kuyashisa* itself, of course, the outward-directed attack is characteristically directed toward oneself at the same time, and it is when this *kuyashisa* is turned still more inward, it seems, that *kuyami* results. Either way, in depression it is chiefly *kuyami* that is to the fore, and there is almost no sense of *kuyashisa*. One does not lapse into depression so long as one can have the *kuyashii* feeling, and it is when the individual is driven into a state where he can no longer even feel *kuyashii* that *kuyami* of a depressive kind begins.

As we have already seen, *kuyami* and *kuyashisa* are not exclusively pathological, but are found also in normal individuals. *Kuyami*, one might say, only becomes depression when it invades the whole spirit. One could also say that an individual's mental state is depressive to the extent that *kuyami* is present. One might formulate the development of this *kuyami* by saying that first there occurs some obstacle to *amae*. The individual tries to arrange things so that he feels better (*ki ga sumu*), but the obsession will not go away (*ki ga sumanai*), and he feels *kuyashii* (an ill-defined sense of personal outrage); if even this proves not to help the result is *kuyamu* (a sense of passive, helpless regret). Since this explanation, however, is rather too schematic, let us consider the process more concretely with reference to the individual who has lost someone close to him.

Recalling his relationship with the deceased, the survivor feels all kinds of regrets. Undoubtedly, this represents a sense of guilt of a kind, but it still leaves something unsatisfactory, in that in his heart of hearts he is regretting being obliged to feel that sense of guilt. Although in appearance self-reproach, it is in some ways a resentment towards the deceased, or, if not the deceased, fate. This—since in his heart he wishes that he did not have to feel guilt—is a kind of *amae*. Yet at the same time, since it is in practice impossible to wipe out the sense of guilt, it can also be thought of as an inability to *amaeru*. In short, he experienced some kind of conflict with the deceased during

124

his lifetime, but managed not to become obsessive (*ki ga sumanai*) about it while the other was still alive. Once the other is dead, however, it is no longer possible to dispose of his feelings (*ki o sumasu*). However "vexed" (*kuyashii*) he feels at not having done some particular thing while the other was still alive, it is now too late. The result is that he surrenders to the emotion of *kuyami*.

Finally, I would like to consider briefly the fact—which should be obvious since *kuyami* and *kuyashisa* are, as the preceding shows, extensions of the *amae* mentality—that the Japanese are particularly prone to this frame of mind. The tendency, so marked in the Japanese, to sympathize with characters such as Hangan in *Chūshingura* is closely related to this. Satō Tadao,[73] who has shown deep insight in discussing this question, states that the strong sense of affinity the Japanese feel for popular heroes such as Yoshitsune, Kusunoki Masashige, the "forty-seven loyal samurai" and Saigō Takamori—all of whom in some way or other suffered misfortune or defeat—is a sign of a kind of moral masochism. I believe this interpretation to be absolutely correct, but the same mentality might be described in more everyday Japanese as a product of *kuyashisa*. The Japanese are very prone to feelings of *kuyashisa*, and oddly enough seem to cherish them, having no thought that the *kuyashii* feeling as such is something repellent. They identify with those historical figures who would seem to have had their fill of such feelings, and by exalting them seek to achieve a catharsis of their own *kuyashisa*.

The same trend makes itself apparent not only toward historical personages but toward contemporary figures as well. As a recent example one might cite the vague sympathy accorded by the public to Zenkyōtō. (In fact, a special term, *shinjō sampa* evolved to mean a sympathiser of the Zenkyōtō movement.) This may be a sign, of course, that the views of Zenkyōtō themselves justify a high degree of public sympathy, but I feel sure there is more to it than that, since even those who vaguely side with Zenkyōtō stop short in most cases of approval for the organization's acts of violence, which they merely accept as something "unavoidable." Whenever the riot police take action against Zenkyōtō because of its acts of violence, there is a general tendency to side with the latter. It is only too obvious that this reaction is stimulated by the overwhelming strength of the riot police in comparison with Zenkyōtō. Most bystanders, in other words, unconsciously identify with the *kuyashisa* which the Zenkyōtō students are presumably feeling, and consequently accord them emotional support even while criticizing them intellectually.

In the sympathy that they accord the emotion of *kuyashisa*, the Japanese would seem to differ considerably from Westerners. The idea of revenge is, of course, present in the West, but whereas revenge there is closely associated with the sense of justice, this is not necessarily the case with Japanese *kuyashisa*. The latter is associated, rather, with *amae*. The *ressentiment* mentality of which talk has been heard in the West in recent years may come somewhat close to *kuyashisa*, but it is held to be an emotion of which one does not care to speak to others, in which respect it affords a strong contrast with the importance attached to *kuyashisa* in Japan. According to Nietzsche, *ressentiment* deriving from the slave outlook lay behind Christianity. Even before Nietzsche, in fact, Kierkegaard—though his views on Christianity are fundamentally different—warned against the damage done by *ressentiment*.[74] In modern times, Max Scheler[75] has discussed *ressentiment* in detail, but, like the rest, critically. It is most significant that the same emotion should receive such totally different appraisals in Japan and in the West, but the reason, surely, depends on the presence or absence of the *amae* mentality.

Even in Japan, the emotion of *kuyashisa* as such is far from being considered pleasant, and people realize that it is frequently the direct cause of morbid states of mind. Yet despite this the emotion is still treated with respect, a fact which can only be attributed ultimately to the affirmative attitude of the Japanese toward *amae*. The people of the West, on the other hand, criticize *ressentiment*, though this does not mean that *ressentiment* thereby disappears—the ideal proof being that Nietzsche who attacked Christianity so vigorously was himself a veritable repository of *ressentiment*. What is interesting, nevertheless, is that modern man in the West is gradually, via the mentality expressed in the term *ressentiment*, drawing closer to the *amae* psychology.

The sense of injury

Another group of words that stands as a symbol of a certain aspect of the Japanese psychology centers on the noun *higai*. This word, written with two Chinese characters signifying respectively "receive" and "harm," was not used in Japanese prior to the Meiji Restoration of 1868, having been newly created as a legal term to indicate the incurred damage (*higai*) or the wronged party (*higaisha*). It was later adopted by psychiatrists as a translation of the German word *Beeintrachtigung* in expressions such as *Beeintrachtigungswahn* (Japanese *higai-mōsō*). What is interesting, now, is that although this new word was originally a technical term it rapidly became acclimatized in popular speech, and gave birth to other expressions such as *higaisha ishiki* (consciousness of having been wronged, sense of grievance), and *higaiteki*. The last word is an adjective (or, with the further addition of the particle *ni*, an adverb) formed by adding the suffix *-teki*, and defies concise translation into English. Thus "to take something *higaiteki ni*" means "to take something (mistakenly) as an attack on or criticism of oneself," "to take something as directed against oneself." To say, for

127

example, "to take something injuriously" would not be good English, even if understandable.

The readiness with which Japanese took over and expanded this term is probably not unrelated to the abundance of expressions already existing in Japanese to indicate the concrete fact of *higai* or receiving harm. One example is the use of the passive in Japanese that was pointed out by Kindaichi Haruhiko.[76] Japanese do not usually say, as English does, "the house was built by a carpenter," but it does say, on the other hand, "we were built a house on our playground"—i.e. someone (to our dismay) went and built a house on our playground —a use of the passive, not to be found in English, which permits expression of the feelings of the children on whose playground the house was built. It is the same with "I was rained on today," another typically Japanese construction. Paralleling this use of the passive to indicate the receipt of harm or injury, the use of expressions showing the receipt or conferring of some benefit is also a conspicuous feature of the Japanese language, and one might see this too as hinting at the state of mind evoked—the sense of grievance or injury—where one has failed to receive some benefit.

Other very convenient expressions indicating the same outlook are *jama sareru* and *jama ga hairu* (to have something one is doing interfered with or impeded by some outside agency). The word *jama* itself, written with the Chinese characters for "evil" and "demon," was originally a Buddhist term that meant, literally, an evil demon that hindered the monk in his religious practices, but at some stage or other its meaning was extended in popular speech to cover almost everything that could possibly disturb the individual's peace of mind. Moreover, by making slight changes in the verb that follows *jama*, one can express all kinds of involved states of mind—for example, *jama suru* (to hinder), *jama ni naru* (to be in the way), or *jama ni suru* (treat as a hindrance or nuisance).

Interest in this linguistic phenomenon once prompted me to write an article in which I touched on the relationship between awareness of *jama* and the *amae* mentality.[77] "The prototype of *amae*," I wrote, "is of course that of the infant; in this case, there is an attempt to monopolize the object of *amae*—the mother—and a strong jealousy toward any diversion of the mother's attention toward others. Other individuals appear as *jama* (objects in the way, hindrances) to him and as such he works to get rid of them. The frequency with which the individual, when he *amaeru's*, has this awareness of *jama* is probably related to the fact that the satisfaction or otherwise of *amae* depends ultimately on the other person, toward whom the individual concerned is adopting an attitude of passive dependence. Since the object of *amae* cannot be completely controlled by oneself the individual concerned is correspondingly likely to get hurt or to have his aims interfered with."

In short, one might say that the sense of being hindered or interfered with—the sense, that is, of being victimized—is closely related to the *amae* mentality, and that it is precisely the dominance of the *amae* mentality in Japanese society that has given rise to such a strong awareness of *jama*. For instance, the same sense of grievance is at work in reactions such as *suneru* and *higamu* already explained (p. 29). Even apart from cases where, as with *jama sareru* and *jama ga hairu*, the sense of being the injured party is made quite plain, a similar sense is lurking in the background in almost all cases where the word *jama* is used. For example, the victimizing mentality of *jama suru* is only the reverse of the victimized mentality of *jama sareru*, and experientially, perhaps, the latter is prior to the former *jama ni suru*. The feeling that something is in the way carries a slight sense of being victimized, and probably coincides with *toraware* (p. 101). Again, the sense that one is "in the way" (*jama ni naru*) is an internalization of the feeling that one is being hindered (*jama sareru*) oneself; since one cannot

129

get rid of the hindrance, one ends up by coming to look on oneself as a hindrance instead.

As we have seen, the "victim mentality" seems to be an extremely everyday underlying component of the Japanese mentality, and a particular phrase, *higaisha ishiki* (sense of being a victim), has been specially coined. This phrase, which does not refer to a temporary sense of grievance but to the sense that one's own social position is itself that of a victim, naturally came into being in response to a felt need. Indeed, Maruyama Masao has pointed out the paradox that those in leading positions in various fields of Japanese society suffer, despite their positions as leaders, from the sense of being victims.[78] Maruyama relates this to the fact that Japanese society has developed, as it were, in a confined space, but surely it could also be seen as originating in the sense of being the injured party —in short, the *amae* mentality—that lies hidden in the Japanese.

Now, the sense of being a victim that I have just discussed applies to the normal individual, and is eminently comprehensible in the light of the human relationships peculiar to the Japanese. Sometimes, however, there occur cases where the sense of injury is extremely clearly defined yet cannot be explained in relation to the circumstances in which the individual finds himself. This is what is known to psychiatrists as a delusion of persecution, and the person who suffers from it considers himself to be the principal victim. The difference from the sense of victimization of the normal person is that with the latter the sense is never held by him alone but is shared with the group to which he belongs, whereas the man suffering from a persecution complex believes that he alone is the victim of some scheme.

The mentality of the person suffering from pathological delusions of victimization may be difficult to understand on the surface, yet understanding is possible if it is seen as, basically, a morbid transformation of the *amae* mentality. The chief proof of this is that the patient is isolated socially and, very often, domestically also. In no small number of cases he has grown up without experiencing what it is to *amaeru* to another person. The chief cause here would seem to be the environment in which he grew up—though in quite a few cases the environment itself would seem to have been fashioned by his own innate oversensitivity. He grows up almost crushed beneath pressures that are invisible to those about him. Even when the time finally comes for him to awaken to his own self, he is unable to be aware of himself as himself. He can apprehend himself only in terms of "being obstructed by someone," "having his brains picked," "being put up to do something," "being managed by someone."

Where this state of affairs is observable, doctors label the case schizophrenia; a comparatively large number of those whose illness begins with these symptoms are young people. In cases where the individual shows signs of the disease only on encountering a particular, dangerous situation and after he has become socially established the illusions of victimization take more concrete forms. He may, for example, see the neighbors whispering among each other and immediately imagine that they are slandering him. Such delusions are often backed up by delusions of grandeur; the patient may suppose that he is being persecuted because he is a person of some special importance. Delusions of persecution and grandeur, it should be added, are not confined to cases diagnosed as schizophrenia, but appear in other types of illness also.

To pursue this further would mean becoming too technical, so I will stop here. The point I wish to make is that most persons who show symptoms of illusions of persecution or grandeur after reaching adulthood have been, from the outset, given to what is known in Japanese as *shūnen*[79] (brooding, especially with feelings of vindictiveness; extraordinary tenaciousness in connection with a particular purpose). This word is rich in

131

implications, and in the phrase *shūnen-bukai* (full of *shūnen*) comes close to expressing the *kuyashii* mentality already discussed. *Shūnen-bukai*, however, goes farther than *kuyashii* in that it carries explicit overtones of revenge-seeking. Where the "revenge" does not originate simply in personal hatred but is moved by the desire to gain victory in some field of competition allowed by society, the same tenacity of purpose may frequently be extolled as admirable (as in the phrase *shūnen no hito*, man of *shūnen*). Now, the man characterized by *shūnen* who is liable to delusions of persecution or grandeur is like a man the object of whose tenacity is unrealistic and who can only be seen as seeking after a vague sense of fulfilment or omnipotence. With such a man it is likely that, even if not totally deprived of the chance to *amaeru* in childhood, he at least never enjoyed it in the true sense. In other words, *amae* has seldom acted as an intermediary via which he could experience empathy with others. His pursuit of *amae* tends to become self-centered, and he seeks fulfilment by becoming one with some object or other that he has fixed on by himself. There develops in him a pronounced tendency to cling to something. If you ask him just why he clings he can give no adequate answer; he does not really know himself. When such a man in the course of life feels that he has encountered some decisive frustration, he may understand the frustration in theory, but he cannot really accept it, and so develops delusions of persecution and grandeur, shutting himself up still more tightly in his shell.

The lack of self

The expression *jibun ga aru*, "to have a self," or *jibun ga nai*, "to have no self" is probably peculiar to Japanese. The Japanese word translated here as "self," *jibun*, is often used in place of first person pronouns such as *watakushi, boku,* or *ore,* to mean simply "I," but it suggests a rather more reflective view of the self than the rest. In terms of the languages of the West, it resembles a reflexive pronoun. For this reason, in sentences such as "he has a *jibun*," or "I have no *jibun*," the question at stake is the presence or absence of this reflective awareness of one's self as an entity. The interesting question, however, is why Japanese should go out of its way to remark on this presence or absence; at least in the West, there is no precise equivalent in other languages for such an expression, though "he has no personality" may come closest to it.

In the languages of the West, the use of the first person pronoun is considered in itself adequate proof of the existence of a self. This raises a number of questions, however, for the use of the first person pronoun does not necessarily imply a clearcut consciousness of the self. Take, for instance, the small child who has only just begun to speak: he may, it is true, already be using the first person pronoun, but it is impossible to believe that he has an objective conception of his own self. Much more unlikely is it in cases where he refers to himself, in the third person, by his own name—a habit which continues in Japan until a comparatively late age. Even in cases such as these, of course, it is probably possible to say with Kant that "Even before men are able to talk about the ego, all languages, in using the first person, are obliged to take the self into consideration.[80] However, this merely means that it is potentially so, and is far from saying that in actual practice the ego is being speculated on in a reflective manner; even where the first person pronoun is in use it is possible for there to be no consciousness of the ego as such. In the West there is a linguistic emphasis on the use of the first person, and the child is awakened to an awareness of the self from a very early age, so that expressions equivalent to *jibun ga nai* have never come into everyday use— the use of expressions similar to it, being confined to clearly

133

abnormal cases, such as schizophrenia. In Japan, on the other hand, the first person pronoun is often omitted, with the converse result, it would seem, of making people clearly aware of this question of the presence or absence of a self.

Let us spend a little time, then, considering just what the expressions *jibun ga aru* and *jibun ga nai* signify in Japanese. One thing, first of all, that is extremely clear is that the two expressions define the relation to his surroundings of the person of whom they are used. "Surroundings" here of course means not the natural scene but the human relationships in which he finds himself, i.e. the group. If the individual is submersed completely in the group, he has no *jibun*. But even where he is not completely submersed in the group—though he may be aware of himself as part of a group and may even, on occasion, recognize with discomfort the existence of a self whose interests do not coincide with those of the group—he does not necessarily have a *jibun*. If he suppresses the discomfort not because of physical compulsion from the group but because his own desire to belong to the group is stronger than the suffering, or if—which comes ultimately to the same thing—his blind loyalty toward the group leads him to keep quiet concerning his differences with the group, then again he must be described as *jibun ga nai*. From this, it should be clear, also, in what cases the expression *jibun ga aru* is appropriate. Its essence does not necessarily lie in rejection of the group; but an individual is said to have a *jibun* when he can maintain an independent self that is never negated by membership of the group.

What is important here is that the real essence of the conflict situation just described lies within the individual himself. In short, the individual wants to make the group's interests accord with his own. But if, when this proves impossible, he tries to champion his own interests he invites charges of being selfish or wilful. In a sense, it is extremely ironic that he should be the subject of such criticism, since even if he wishes to manage

134

things to suit his own interests, it will normally be impossible. Not only is it impossible for him to get his way in practice, but his failure creates a deep hurt in his own mind, for the group for him is basically a vital spiritual prop, to be isolated from which would be, more than anything else, to lose his "self" completely in a way that would be intolerable to him. He is obliged, therefore, to choose to belong to the group even at the cost of temporary obliteration of his self. In fact, this is no different essentially from the *giri-ninjō* conflict described earlier (p. 33). Just as the *giri-ninjō* conflict is rooted ultimately in *amae*, so the conflict between the individual and the group would seem essentially to derive from the *amae* of the individual.

As the preceding consideration will show, the traditional importance attached in Japan to *giri* rather than *ninjō*, to the group rather than the individual, may seem at first glance eminently reasonable. By his very nature man seeks the group, and cannot survive without it. If the rejection of the "small self" in favor of the "larger self" is extolled as a virtue, it becomes easier for him to act in concert with the group. In this way friction in human relations within the group is kept to a mimimum, and the efficiency of group activity enhanced. It is this, chiefly, that accounts for the way the Japanese have been able since ancient times to pull together in times of national danger. In the same way, the rapid modernization that startled the West following the Meiji Restoration, and the energy which, following the end of World War II, raised Japan within a quarter of a century from exhaustion to a position as one of the world's great economic powers, were both due, not only to the willingness to adapt and assimilate that we saw in chapter two, but also to the ease with which the national effort can be bent towards a single end. Even EXPO '70, held in Osaka, can be seen as a display of the same national characteristic, both in the way in which all the governmental agencies concerned joined in pressing ahead with preparations and in the fact that, once the exhibition opened, approximately half the nation's population went to see it. Another expression of the same trait may be seen in the general dislike of the Japanese for any conflict of opinions and their liking for at least an appearance of consensus when any decision has to be taken.

At first glance, this trait would undoubtedly seem to bear desirable fruit. But this does not mean that it can be approved without reservation. For it frequently happens—as is implied in the expression "mob psychology"—that the group is moved by the lowest common denominator of possible motives, so that if a complete muzzle is placed on the individual's resistance, all roads are closed to him apart from blindly following suit or servility to the masses. In such a case, men tend to behave like people in a crowded streetcar that too suddenly starts or stops. Unable to withstand the sudden pressure, they cannot on the other hand simply allow themselves to be pushed along without resistance, so without realizing it they find themselves shoving strongly in the direction in which they are being pushed. This is why a crowded tram can be a dangerous source of sudden disaster—and precisely the same kind of thing can happen in a society where effective resistance to the group by the individual is not permitted. It is this kind of phenomenon that is meant by the term mass hysteria. Individual hysteria is an attempt by the individual to have his own way, and the group that does not allow the individual to have his own way is itself liable to give way, as a group, to hysterical behavior.

A word here about hysteria: it refers to cases in which the motive for the individual's behavior is to attract the attention of those about him and which frequently involve extreme actions, the subject all the while keeping an eye on what is happening about him. Although this might seem "self-centered" in its attempt to focus attention on the self, it indicates not the presence of a true self but a fear that unless the sub-

136

ject behaves in this way he cannot be sure of his own existence at all. To use an expression that Natsume Sōseki coined in a lecture on "The Westernization of Modern Japan," it may be called "moving in response to external rather than internal motives." Since they are external, if the circumstances in which the subject finds himself suddenly change, he too must change, with a result that he is prone to sudden enthusiasms and equally sudden coolings-off. In other words, he may blindly acquiesce in something one day, only quite blithely to go along with something different the next day.

Although the foregoing refers to individual hysteria, much the same thing may, I believe, be said of mass hysteria. A good example is afforded by the university disputes that caused such a stir in Japan a few years back. These did not occur entirely without justification, of course, and cannot therefore be dismissed simply as a pathological phenomenon, but it is undeniable that what happened involved a considerable amount of hysteria. I refer to the way in which the dispute spread like wildfire to other universities, rapidly gathering supporters and plunging the university world into chaos—only to subside just as rapidly in sensitive response to the political situation outside the universities. One university professor commented on how odd it was to see students who, only a year previously, had walked out of classes in their zeal to reform the universities now studiously attending their lectures as though the reform movement had never existed.

It is, indeed, odd. The phenomenon cannot be explained entirely by saying that the barriers to reform had proved insurmountable. One is reminded strongly that the same nation which after the outbreak of the last war rose as one man in an all-out struggle against the "American and British beasts" switched overnight, once the war ended, to pro-American and pro-British eulogies of democracy.

So far, I have tried to explain the absence of a "self" in terms of the individual's submersion in or submission to the group. However, mention should also be made of the opposite case, where the individual develops a sense of having no self as a result of being totally isolated from the group. So strongly, one might say, do people fear such a state of affairs that they will usually put up with anything in order to belong to a group.

A recent episode affecting myself personally may help to illustrate this. It happened when I was put under pressure by a group of young doctors to explain what I was doing about the many anomalies in the Japanese medical system. The trouble arose when I resigned from a hospital with which I had hitherto been connected in protest against an incident for which I personally had no direct responsibility. My decision was made in the hope of making clear where the responsibility lay and at the same time encouraging the executive of the hospital to apply its whole energies to the solution of the problem for which it had direct responsibility. My logic, however, failed entirely to get over to the younger doctors. Why, they asked, did I not use my influence in an attempt to get at the situation in hand; not to do so, they said, was running away. I accepted their criticisms meekly, whereupon one of them asked me if I would behave in the same way if a similar incident occurred at the other hospital with which I was connected. I thought for a while and replied that I probably would; if the worst came to the worst, I added, I could always go into practice on my own account. "But that would mean losing your identity completely, wouldn't it?" said one of them with a hopelessly puzzled expression.

I repeat this story, not in the attempt to justify my own approach, but because I think that the young doctor's last remark gets at the very heart of the question. The word "identity" used here can be taken as the equivalent of *jibun*. As for myself, I did not care if I was isolated or even if people said that I had run away, being more interested in seeing the execu-

138

tive of the hospital, which had so far depended on its relationship with me, stand on its own feet. But as the young doctors saw it, to be isolated was the same as losing one's very self.

It is true that loss of the world to which one belongs is normally experienced as a loss of the self. There have been patients who related to me their experience of such a loss with every sign of anxiety, and others who described their own state of mind on losing some affiliation in the following terms: "One is like a single dot; there is nothing to which one belongs—no class, no family, no occupation." One could quote any number of similar expressions. For example, "I can see my own mind, but I can't get hold of it. When I try to get hold of it sinks out of sight." "I feel as if I were about to lose my identity (*jibun*), as though I couldn't distinguish between myself and others." "I've no self to go back into." Cases such as those discussed earlier in connection with the sense of being wronged, in which the patient has a sense of being hindered, having his brains picked, or being "managed" also represent, it seems, the same kind of "lack of self" state. The statements just quoted were, incidentally, all made by patients diagnosed as schizophrenic, and differ from cases where the individual loses his self through being submerged in the group. Schizophrenic patients lose their identity through total isolation from the group; the things they say are frequently dismissed as bizarre, yet the experience that lies behind their remarks reveals a law that lies at the very foundation of human existence: that man cannot lead a human kind of existence without the experience of having belonged to something or other.

To express what has just been said in different terms, man cannot possess a self without previous experience of *amaeru*. As we have already seen, submersion in the group means loss of the self, but this does not mean, conversely, that to behave selfishly without submersing oneself in the group is enough to produce a self. The crucial point is that to try to have one's own way exclusively is to come up against the barrier of reality and develop hysteria. What, then, of the man who seeks to go along with the trend and submits blindly to the group? This is no good either; indeed, this kind of approach sometimes poisons the group to which the individual belongs and leads to mass hysteria. It is, in short, extremely difficult to have a "self."

In what I have said here, I have been dealing mostly with the Japanese, but this is only because the problem can be observed in a peculiarly clear form in the Japanese, and does not imply that the difficulty in attaining a sure personal identity is necessarily restricted to them. Assuming, though, that the awareness of "having a self" is easier for the Westerner than the Japanese, it must be because there is something in the Western tradition that causes the individual to transcend the group; something that can transcend the group while giving the individual a sure sense of belonging. I shall not say any more about this here, since I have already discussed the point in the section on *amae* and freedom. Either way, in the West the absence of a self is not considered a virtue as in Japan—though it seems that as a result in the West one finds a completely reverse phenomenon in which the individual while in his heart of hearts harboring an extremely complex feeling toward the "absence of self," or being in some cases aware, essentially, that he has no "self," behaves as though he does in in fact have one.

The awareness of the problem of the "organization man" of which there has been much talk in the West in recent years is extremely interesting here. Since people in the West usually give the individual precedence over the group, they like to believe that they are inwardly free of the group and in no way subservient to it. They all belong, of course, to some group or other, but it is held that this represents a free and voluntary association that can be broken whenever the individual so desires. One of the most typical symbols of this is the various types of social club. This system of social clubs, which has scarcely been developed at all in Japan, is a good illustration of this characteristic of Western man, who has recently been complaining increasingly that without realizing it he is being turned into an "organization man." I know little of the social conditions that form the background to this question; probably the problem is partly attributable to the machinery of capitalist society and the bureaucratic organization. It may also be related to the way the individual in today's post-industrial society finds himself caught in a complex ring of nets. More than these, however, I feel that the new awareness of the question of "organization man" reflects a subtle psychological change that seems to be taking place in Western man.

In short, despite the precedence he gives in theory to the individual over the group, there must exist inside him a psychological desire to "belong." This is, in other words, *amae*. And this desire, one suspects, is gradually coming to the surface of the consciousness now that the Western faith in freedom of the individual is breaking down. He views this fact, however, with mixed feelings. He fears that if this state of affairs goes on developing it will lead to loss of identity—which is why the warning has gone out concerning the "organization man."

5 *Amae* and modern society

Youth and rebellion

The rebellion of youth and the generation gap are a world-wide focus of attention today, and are generally regarded as among the most pressing problems facing society. I propose next to examine this question in the light of the *amae* mentality; if this mentality were exclusively Japanese, the world-wide nature of the two just-mentioned phenomena would suggest that there was little point in doing so, but although the *amae* psychology is particularly marked in the Japanese, in whom it comes to form a world of meaning in itself, it can also serve as a peculiarly convenient means of measuring other things as well. Moreover, the development of communications in the world today means that something that happens in one part of the world is immediately reported all over the globe, and its influence is almost simultaneous. The almost global aspect assumed by the rebellion of youth may surely be attributed in large measure to the fact that, technologically, the world has become one; what is true of rebellion in Japan must also apply to some extent to youth in other countries. The *amae* psychology presents an excellent vantage point from which to understand the problems perplexing the contemporary world. It is precisely in the hope of doing this that I am writing this chapter, but before going further I would like to quote in full my paper on "The Psychology of Today's Rebellious Youth," since though written three years ago it sums up more or less all I wish to say on the subject. I shall follow it with a somewhat more detailed discussion of the main points made in the text.

"The student movement that by now has boiled over on a nationwide scale has been explained in a hundred different ways. Some people, preoccupied with the possible revision of the U.S.-Japanese Security Treaty in 1970, see the students of today as a vanguard of the champions of democracy. Others hold that the old university system has failed to keep up with the postwar changes in Japanese society. Others again see the wilder excesses of the students as marking the failure of the 'democratic education' which has been in force during the twenty-odd years since the end of the war. What should be realized, however, is that the rebellion of youth is a phenomenon that is not confined to Japan but is occurring on a worldwide scale, without regard to ideological differences. Its aim, it would seem, goes further than any overturning of a particular political regime or reform of the university system, lying rather in an arraignment of the whole generation in charge of the world at the moment by those who will form the next generation. It may be that the blame for the failure of education—if one may call it that—does not lie with the educational policies of a political country at a political period, i.e. of postwar Japan, but with all adults in the modern society.

"As early as the years following the end of World War I, the philosopher Ortega y Gasset[81] applied the concept of generations to the interpretation of history, claiming that a rebellion against the tyranny of reason in modern times was already getting under way. Highly thought-provoking though his theories are, to expound them here is not my task. I should like, however, to try simply to relate his theories to the question of the generations as dealt with in my own field of psychiatry.

"For example, the Oedipus complex which Freud considered to be the root of all neurosis, can also be seen as a kind of conflict between the generations. When the conflict is progressively resolved so that the child achieves spiritual identifi-

143

cation with the parents, the way is open for it to become a normal adult—assuming, that is, that the parents and the society they represent are healthy. However, even where the child appears to have identified with its parents and grown into a normal adult, the existence beneath the surface of lingering childhood conflicts can be a source of neurosis. It sometimes happens, furthermore, that the parents do not get on together on account of unhealthy tendencies on one side or the other, so that instead, an unnaturally strong bond forms between one of the parents and the child. In such a case one has, not a conflict between generations such as is represented by the Oedipus complex, but what might be called a loss of the barrier between the generations—which as Dr. Theodore Lidz[82], a long-time student of this problem, has pointed out, is precisely the type of family relationship that can produce the schizophrenic.

"Can these psychiatric theories of the generations throw any light on the question of modern youth? Modern youth is in violent revolt against existing society, and shows a strong mistrust of the older generation. However, this is a social phenomenon observable mainly in the macrocosm; when one examines individual family relationships, one begins to suspect that there is little emotional antagonism between parent and child after all. Though youth talks a great deal of the generation gap, there is little actual evidence of dispute between the two sides. In some cases, even, it looks very much as though there is collusion. The relationship, in other words, is one of *amae* and the permitting of *amae*, with no feeling of paternal authority. It would almost seem as though modern youth has not passed through the classic generation conflict postulated by Freud.

"While considering such matters, I was reminded of the story of Momotarō, so beloved of Japanese children. For all his closeness to his parents, Momotarō could not identify with them; he found something unsatisfactory about the parents who had

144

found and raised him. When he grew up, however, he discovered a goal in life—the conquest of Demon Island—toward
which he could direct the feelings he could not direct toward
his parents, and thanks to which he was transformed into an
adult, full of adult self-confidence. For him, the conquest of the
demons was a kind of initiation into adulthood.

"The more I reflect on this Momotarō story, the more strongly
I feel the resemblance to modern youth. For young people today, their parents are much the same as the old man and old
woman in the tale: they receive protection and love from them,
but no advice on how to grow up into adulthood; they do not
know, even, in what way their parents, as adults, are different
from themselves. So they too, like Momotarō, require some
Demon Island on which to expend their energies. Some years
back, an actual enemy without provided the ideal object of
this kind. But the world today provides scarcely so much as a
hypothetical enemy; this is as true of America and the other
advanced nations as it is of Japan. So demons are no longer
found overseas, but among those in power at home. This is the
enemy against whom they are pitching their youthful passions.

"Although they are driven psychologically to find demons to
conquer in the manner of Momotarō, there is one respect in
which they differ from him. In the Momotarō story, the hero's
conquest of the demons is received with joy by his parents also,
and everybody lives happily ever after; but things are different
with modern youth. There are, of course, some adults who
privately support the young people in the hope that they will
achieve what they themselves failed to do. But the situation is
too serious to admit of such romantic dreams, for there is a real
danger that in their zeal to conquer demons the young people
will become demons themselves.

"Generally speaking, when youth becomes over-confident
about its own strength, it tends to become indistinguishable
from the forces it is attacking. What it is really seeking is a test

145

THE ANATOMY OF DEPENDENCE

of its own strength that will teach it its limitations.

"But who is to give it such a chance in today's society? Who can be a father to it and teach it anew the meaning of authority and order? Not the university professors, certainly, nor the politicians, nor the intellectuals, nor the men of religion . . . On this score, the modern age offers no hope at all. The anarchy of today is not, in truth, the anarchy of a handful of young people, but of the whole spirit of the age; which being so, it seems likely that modern youth is going to go on testing its own strength for a long time to come."

Modern man's sense of alienation

The present age is one of crisis and upheaval. It may be that, in passing through crisis and upheaval, the world is gathering itself together in one particular direction that will eventually lead to a new age. Some, indeed, might take the view that that new age has already arrived. Yet many people view this new age with a deep apprehension: are these changes really desirable, they ask, for the sake of mankind? Thus the facile slogan "Peace and prosperity for mankind" chosen for EXPO '70, held in Osaka, struck many people as empty rhetoric. Indeed, to judge from the actual world about us, the civilization now in the course of evolution creates an excessive number of contradictions and evils.

It is a primitive awareness of this, one imagines, that is driving today's youth into revolt. If possible, youth wants to halt the flow of history. It is quite prepared, if necessary, to destroy contemporary civilization. But this is, culturally, impossible. Far from stopping the flow of history, youth tends to find itself caught up in turn in the swirling current and carried onward willy-nilly. Almost certainly it senses this somewhere in its heart—which is why, it seems, it feels obliged to become drop-outs, or hippies, or to indulge in the desperate, self-destructive activities of the New Left.

The term "the alienation of man" has become almost a cliché in describing this contemporary situation. The word alienation, originally used in a special sense by Hegel, was adopted by Marx for his own purposes, and further modified for use in its current broad sense. I will leave detailed exposition of the term to other works, however, and instead put forward a few ideas on why this term "human alienation" should have become so popular.

First of all, where man once felt pride in the modern civilization created by science and technology, he has now come to fear its ever-accelerating advances. He cherishes the suspicion that in return for civilization he is being deprived of something irreplaceable. This emotional reaction had occurred before the atomic bomb and long before people awoke to the problem of pollution about which one hears so much these days. Natsume Sōseki, via the character of Ichirō in his novel *Kōjin*, expressed this fear in extremely acute terms: "Man's anxiety stems from the development of science. Science, advancing without pause, has never permitted us to pause, even for a while. From walking to the jinrikisha, from the jinrikisha to the horse carriage, from the horse carriage to the streetcar, from the streetcar to the automobile, then the airship, then the aeroplane, on and on, never allowing one to stop and rest. No one can tell just where we shall end up. It is terrifying."

As for the true nature of this fear, the ideas of Ortega y Gasett, whom I mentioned earlier, are extremely illuminating here. He starts with the fundamental fact that human life depends on the change of generations. All human life, in other words, has its own law that says that every generation must start, as it were, from scratch. For that reason, human life can never be completely dominated either by revealed faith or by pure reason. Just as during the Renaissance pure reason arose

147

in defiance of revelation, so today life itself is seeking to recover its natural rights from the grasp of pure reason. Such, in brief, is Ortega's theory. However, it may not be easily under stood, since one could argue as follows: that man, feeling himself to be dominated by revealed faith, should have risen against it is understandable, yet why should man have to object in the same way to being dominated by pure reason? Why should one go so far as to blame reason for the alienation of human existence? Surely reason is something of man's own? Was not the joyous sense of recovery of the self that the Renaissance gave to men due above all to its championship of free reason exercised by man himself as opposed to the authority of revealed faith?

The answer to this question, one might say, is implicit in the question itself; for contemporary alienation has its ultimate origin in the discovery that man was mistaken in believing, since the dawn of the modern age, that he could stand on his own feet and be self-sufficient through reason alone. Interestingly enough, Goethe had a presentiment of this as early as the beginning of the nineteenth centurv. His Faust appears as a Renaissance man, but unlike the actual Renaissance man he does not exude confidence and joy; rather, he is sick of thought and study. Despairing of the self, he determines to end his life by taking poison. He is deterred by the sound of an Easter hymn, yet this does not mean that his faith has been reborn; indeed, he only realizes afresh his own lack of faith, and it is the recollections of happy childhood invoked by the hymn that make him give up his idea of suicide. Casting prudence to the winds, he abandons himself to all the temptations that Mephistopheles can provide. Yet, despite this, he still dies without having experienced true satisfaction; and as he dies Goethe has a heavenly choir sing: "*Das Ewig-Weibliche zieht uns hinan.*"

Might one not see in this a symbol of the progress of the

soul of modern man? Modern man too, having tried everything in reliance on reason, is beginning to despair of the self.
Beyond doubt, scientific civilization has flaunted the power
of man for all to see; yet this no longer, as it once did, serves
man as an inspiration. Men sense a drying-up of the springs
of life, and in order to recover what has been lost they determine that they will return, as it were, to their naked selves,
will live once more by feeling rather than reason. And in this
new quest they are being led, it seems, just as is suggested in
the closing lines of *Faust*, to the maternal—in other words, to
amae.

If one examines the question from the viewpoint of the
sensibility of the new generation in contact with contemporary
civilization, one comes up against a similar sense of alienation.
In contact with the vast and complex machinery of modern
civilization, the new generation, one suspects, experiences an
emotion close to fear or awe, much as an ignorant savage
might. This is particularly true now that the destruction of the
environment by civilization has been shown to be so serious.
The new generation sees modern civilization as a product of
the same intellect that it shares itself, but it cannot identify
with it. Those responsible for running contemporary civilization tend for the most part to assume that the workings of
reason that underpin its development are self-evident, but
this assumption itself is not necessarily true. The younger
generation feels an instinctive threat in modern civilization; to
quote again from Sōseki: "The world," just as Sanshirō found
it when he came to Tokyo from the country, "is obviously in
an upheaval. One is witness to the upheaval, but one can have
no part in it. One's own world and the world of actuality
lie on the same plane, but nowhere do they touch. Thus the
world heaves and moves on, leaving one behind. It is most
disturbing."

It is obvious that this sense of being left behind depends on

149

the existence of the *amae* mentality. When the infant is left by its mother, it feels an uneasiness, a threat to its very life; and it seems likely that it is precisely this feeling that lies at the heart of what is described by modern man as "human alienation."

The fatherless society

The term "generation gap" has become a cliché by now. On countless different scores the older generation is being called to account by the new, so that the two sides would seem to have lost any common ground for understanding. Yet if one examines the phenomenon in detail one begins to suspect that the struggle between the two is primarily for public consumption, and that within the home parent and child get along better than one might think. For example, a poll of the views of students of Tokyo University carried out recently by the *Asahi Shimbun* showed that the list of persons they most respected was headed by their mothers. Another pointer in the same direction is the fact that during the annual May festival held at the height of the recent Tokyo University disturbances, a placard was borne aloft bearing the legend "Don't stop us, Mother, the ginko trees* are weeping." Presumably the students felt that their mothers, if no one else, would know how they felt.

This private tie between activist youth and the mother had in fact already been demonstrated ten years previously in the case of the students active in the struggle against revision of the U.S.–Japanese Security Treaty. Professor Robert Lifton[83] of Yale University was in Japan at the time; he had interviews with a number of these activists, and I listened to the tapes with him. They all suggested a very close connection between

---

* i.e. the university is in dire trouble, a reference to the gingko trees that grow in large numbers on the Tokyo University campus.

those interviewed and their mothers. I heard the same kind of thing recently from Professor Toussieng, who lectures on child psychiatry at the University of Oklahoma. He and his colleagues made a survey of children of predominantly conservative families living in Topeka City, Kansas, and discovered that while clearly advocating views different from those of their parents, on the human level they felt no enmity towards the latter; if anything, they tended to show respect and gratitude.

In other words, contemporary youth will go along with the older generation so long as its sense of values is not at stake, but opposes it sharply once that sense is called into question. This, presumably, is precisely why they continue a closer relationship with their mothers than their fathers. True, within the home itself there does not seem to be much conflict even with the father, who normally stands for the established values of society; this is probably because very few fathers nowadays attempt to educate their children in any sense of values. These fathers, too, have in their own hearts a sense of alienation; they instinctively feel that modern society is in a crisis, and as such are the last to want to imbue their children with accepted values. Yet at the same time they are, socially, in a position of having to defend the system or organization to which they belong. It would seem that the modern conflict between the generations is chiefly in the public sector, and is waged in the form of system versus system.

An odd fact here is that although the conflict, or gap, between the generations would seem, as we have seen already, to have arisen mainly in connection with senses of values, the difference between the rival sets of values is not always clear. The older generation, in the first place, does not necessarily subscribe to the old values. The majority, if anything, are suspicious of them. The new generation, on the other hand, is not offering any new set of values. If this is so, then the present conflict

151

between the generations, though ostensibly concerned with values, cannot be said in fact to focus on them. Why, then, should the younger generation attack the old? In some ways, the attack might be seen as attempting to force the older generation to reveal its true feelings. In short, the younger generation hopes to acquire a set of values according to which it can live, and it is irritated at the older generation's failure to provide one. This could doubtless be called a kind of *amae*, though it seems unlikely that to say that today's youth are indulging in *amae* is going to be enough to resolve the generation gap.

There are grounds for believing, in short, that the question of the generation gap today has its origins in the older generation's loss of self-confidence. At the ordinary domestic level, this reveals itself in that the father's influence has declined almost to the point where it ceases to exist. One of the problems affecting children that attracted general attention following the end of the war in Japan was the phenomenon referred to as "school phobia," or refusal to attend school, and surveys of the families concerned show that the father was consistently a weak figure. This observation, however, is not restricted to families where the children refuse to attend school, but is a common characteristic of modern society as a whole.

Another parallel social phenomenon could be seen in the fact that although power nowadays has become increasingly concentrated and extremely potent, there is nothing to convey a true sense of authority. It might, thus, be possible to lump the two phenomena together and characterize modern society as a society "without a father." This expression "fatherless society" was first used, to the best of my knowledge, by Paul Federn, a pupil of Freud, in his *On the Psychology of Revolution: The Fatherless Society*[84], published in 1919. As the title suggests, it was prompted by the political situation in Europe following

World War I, but the social changes that have occurred since then have only made the expression more apt than ever.

The seeds of these social changes had already been sown, in a sense, during the nineteenth century, by men such as Darwin, Marx, and Nietzsche, each of whom smashed value norms that had been subscribed to previously, thereby preparing the way for the social upheaval to come. Japan too, although the historical circumstances were utterly different, would seem in a sense to have become, since the Meiji Restoration, a "fatherless society," insofar as all existing order and authority, with the exception of the emperor system, was overthrown when Western civilization was introduced. The somewhat old-fashioned ring that the word *oyaji* (the old man) now has (along with its overtones of affection) is probably a reflection of what happened during this period. Even so, until the end of the last war the father was still something to be looked up to. With the end of the war, he rapidly ceased even to be respected, one reason being that the defeat dealt an even more decisive blow to the old morality. Shortly after Japan's defeat, the loyalty-filial-piety ethic that had hitherto lain at the heart of the national spirit was subjected to criticism from all sides. At the same time, the West itself, hitherto looked up to as "advanced," fell prey to postwar chaos, and the whole world drifted further and further, ideologically speaking, towards the rejection of paternal authority.

A word here concerning the connection between Freudian psychoanalysis and the social changes just referred to: Freud's ideas are usually ranked with those of Marx and Nietzsche as having aided and encouraged the social changes in process today. It is true that his claim that the human mind is dominated by the unconscious, and that there is a profound inner relationship between the higher workings of the mind and the instinctive life had an incalculable effect in revolutionizing the outlook of modern man. But just as the chief characteristic of the psychoanalysis he created was not merely to analyse the patient's psychology but by analysis to change it, so the social influence exerted by his work occurred via analysis of the social outlook. On no occasion, of course, did Freud discuss the phenomenon of the fatherless society in the form in which I am discussing it here, but even so he did touch on it in one sense— in the constantly recurring theme of patricide, which, I feel sure, is related to it.

Freud, in short, interprets absence of the father not simply as such but as a result of patricide. He does not, though, treat this as something in the present, but projects it into human prehistory.[85] It is here that the first Oedipus known to man is performed, though it differs from the countless Oedipuses represented thereafter in human history in that the father is, in actuality, killed. It served nevertheless, according to Freud, to inspire in the children who survived a sense of guilt from which sprang religion and morality. Freud applies the same theme to Moses—in a sense the father of Judaism—and attributes a great significance to the legend of the killing of Moses. There is no need here to defend Freud for any lack of historical proof for his theories; what is important is that he replaced the term "absence of the father" with the term "patricide." And he saw patricide as the foundation of all morality.

Freud, in fact, may be said to have been obsessed all his life by the theme of the father. He is often called the "father" of psychoanalysis, and there is reason to suspect[86] that he liked to see this not simply as a metaphor but as indicating that he was, indeed, a father for mankind in the new age. It is interesting in this connection that whereas the role of the father in Freud's Oedipus complex is extremely great, the men who rejected his theory and attached chief importance to the role of the mother-child relationship in forming the personality were all, including not only Jung but Rank, Ferenczi, and the later neo-Freudians, agreed in presenting their ideas as a denial of their ideological father, Freud. In short, the theory of no father was itself not born without a father, but through rejection of the father. Doubtless Freud himself saw in this another repetition of the eternal motif of patricide.

I suspect that something similar applies to the so-called "fatherless society" of today. Marcuse,[87] who has had such a great influence on the young people of today, sees the fatherless society as a *fait accompli* and speaks as though we need only get rid of the repressive social machinery that still survives today in order to achieve an ideal state resembling the happy identity of mother and child. If Freud were still alive, however, he would almost certainly make a prompt objection to this. Almost certainly, he would write another *Future of an Illusion* attacking the present age's psychoanalytic-socialistic illusions.

The question resolves itself into that of whether the father, or the paternal principle, is redundant or not. Is it really something that could disappear so simply off the face of the earth? I myself cannot think so. Already Federn, in the work just mentioned, seems to have been saying that despite the marked retreat that the father-child motif has been obliged to make in the present age it remains so deeply rooted in human nature that the appearance of a totally "fatherless" society is probably impossible. This has been borne out to a certain extent by the rebellion of youth in recent years, since this can be interpreted as indignation at paternal weakness and an appeal for a stronger father. Mao Tse-tung's appeal for youth all over the world may be a reflection of this state of mind. Generally speaking, revolution represents a psychological slaying of the father, yet oddly enough it often ends by creating a new and stronger father figure—as is clear from the Russian worship of Lenin and the Vietnamese eulogies of Ho Chi-Minh. Even outside communist society, the father figure remains important. It was an appreciation of this that gave de Gaulle his

155

hold over the French public, and the emotion felt not only by the whole of France but by other nations as well when he died in retirement following political defeat can be seen as grief at the death of a great father figure.

Any enlightened contemporary could tell you, of course, that the Great Father is a hollow image, a feeble human no different inside from anyone else. Though Lenin, or Mao Tse-tung may be worshiped at the moment as immortals, they are, nonetheless, fictions. Even in communist society, where the greatest faith is reposed in such fictions, the day will inevitably come when they collapse. If so, why does humanity seek so persistently after the mighty father? Freud's theory of patricide is extremely suggestive here, since it hints that the efforts to find the father spring from a desire to wipe out the memory of patricide. All revolutions can be seen as a repetition of this universal human theme. Man cannot, in the long run, get away from it. Thus, visions of a fatherless utopia inspired by Marcuse will probably prove to be no more than daydreams. The only way, it would seem, of overcoming the present spiritual state of fatherlessness would be to admit the guilt of patricide and make this the basis of a new morality.

At the religious level, the theme of fatherlessness just discussed is a question of the absence of God, so I should like to say something on this point too. Ever since Nietzsche issued his prophetic statement "God is dead," the age has come increasingly to take the absence of God for granted; recently, indeed, there has even been talk of a theology of God's death. This is of course outside my field, but I would point out that Nietzche did not merely say that God was dead, but that God had been killed. This fact, which seems to be surprisingly little known generally, seems to me extraordinarily interesting for its correspondence with Freud's ideas on patricide. Nor can I help feeling that it hints at ideas far more profound than those expounded by today's "theology of God's death." Be that as it may, I will quote the relevant passage from Nietzsche in full. It seems probable that the interpretation of Freud's ideas on patricide that I have given can also be applied to Nietzsche's deicide.

"Have you ever heard of the madman who on a bright morning lighted a lantern and ran to the market place calling out unceasingly: 'I seek God! I seek God!'? As there were many people standing about who did not believe in God, he caused a great deal of amusement. 'Why! is he lost?' said one. 'Has he strayed away like a child?' said another. 'Or does he keep himself hidden?' 'Is he afraid of us?' 'Has he taken a sea voyage?' 'Has he emigrated?' the people cried out laughingly, all in a hubbub. The insane man jumped into their midst and transfixed them with his glances. 'Where is God gone?' he called out. 'I mean to tell you! We have killed him—you and I! We are all his murderers! But how have we done it? How were we able to bring up the sea? . . . Whither do we move? . . . Do we not dash on unceasingly? Backward, sideways, forward, in all directions? Is there still an above and below? Do we not stray, as through infinite nothingness? Does not empty space breathe upon us? Has it not become colder? Does not night come on continually, darker and darker? Shall we not have to light lanterns in the morning? Do we not hear the noise of the gravediggers who are burying God? . . . God is dead! God remains dead! And we have killed him! . . . The holiest and the mightiest that the world has hitherto possessed has bled to death under our knife—who will wipe the blood from us? With what water could we cleanse ourselves? . . . Shall we not ourselves have to become Gods, merely to seem worthy of it? There never was a greater event, and on account of it, all who are born after us belong to a higher history than any history hitherto!' Here the madman was silent and looked again at his hearers; they also were silent and looked at him in surprise."[88]

157

The sense of guilt, the sense of solidarity and the feeling of being victimized

Paternal authority today has receded entirely into the background, and no one ventures to blame the individual for "doing his own thing." Taboos have been swept aside, and the whole of society has a frivolous air. Dealing with the incident, already mentioned, in which Tokyo University students barricaded themselves in the Yasuda Auditorium of the university, the *Asahi Shimbun's* "Vox Populi Vox Dei" column had the following to say: "Strip off the outer layer, and one finds a nation of considerable compassion, where people presume on (*amaeru*) and make allowances for (*amayakasu*) each other in a way that belies the surface rowdiness and hatred. The fight-to-the-last-man poses and the misplaced sympathy for the underdog are, in a sense, a sign of a peaceful country." The predominance of *amae* that this suggests may, admittedly, be particularly marked in Japan. Yet it does seem that the phenomenon is not confined to Japan; a French psychoanalyst[89] said of the "May Revolution" in Paris in 1967 that it was a magical act, an attempt to avoid the Oedipus situation by denying the father without clashing with him in actuality, and that it would never lead to reform.

It would be wrong of course to think that it is only youth that *amaeru* today. Adults too do it in their own way; in a sense, the whole point of the "Vox Populi Vox Dei" article is that the nation as a whole is wallowing in a mood of *amae*. It sometimes happens nowadays that *amae* or related words appear in headlines to newspaper articles. Those I have seen myself, for example, include "Don't expect too much of the Goverment." "Don't take the defense of the dollar lightly," and "Don't take the consumer for granted." Very recently, when

158

negotiations with the U.S. on the textile issue ended unfavorably for Japan, articles appeared stating that Japanese observers had been *amai*, i.e. facilely optimistic concerning the outcome, and shortly after this the Minister of International Trade and Industry was reported as saying, "What I would particularly like to point out here is that (Japan) must stop assuming that everything will go as it wishes (literally, must stop *amaeru*-ing) just because it is dealing with America." Admittedly, it is rather doubtful just how serious warnings such as these are; at the most, the feeling seems to resemble the fond tut-tutting of a parent whose child behaves in a spoilt way, and as such has, itself, an aura of *amae*.

Now, with a society in which everybody is allowed to *amaeru*, one might expect everyone, at least insofar as his subjective feelings are concerned, to be *medetai* and happy, yet oddly enough this is not the case. Modern man is gay and carefree, yet on the other hand seems to be suffering from some vague sense of guilt. Perhaps the clearest expression of this feeling is to be found among the activists of the New Left. They appeal strongly to man's sense of solidarity with his fellow-men. They stress that it is a crime to stand silently by and watch the sufferings of others, whether in Indo-China, the Middle East, or anywhere else, whether abroad or at home. In practice, however, it is not so easy as all that to assuage human suffering, a fact which sharpens their sense of guilt still further. They conclude therefore that the root of all these evils lies in a vast and repressive social organization, on which they launch a bold assault. Anyone who fails to awaken to a similar sense of fellowship and join in their struggle is their enemy. The question, in short, is one of "solidarity" or "fellow-feeling," and it is very interesting in this respect that Oda Makoto[90] of Beheiren,*

---

* The "Peace for Vietnam Committee," a movement started in Japan in 1965 and devoted entirely to opposition to the war in Vietnam. It was especially noted for the aid it gave to deserters from the American forces.

writing in the *Asahi Shimbun* series "The Japan Inside Me," speaks of the sense of comradeship that he felt for American deserters from Vietnam in the following terms: "If I have a 'Japan,' or at least a 'my Japan,' it does not exist apart from such ties (of shared humanity), and those ties, I would insist, can include within themselves such out-of-the-ordinary beings as deserters."

Now these attitudes adopted by the New Left are, considered in themselves, impeccably humanist—with an odor, almost, of Christianity. Its ranks do, in fact, include some earnest Christians, and the same trend is apparently to be found not only in Japan but also in other countries where the New Left is active. There are Christian thinkers, too, who show a considerable sympathy for the movement; the spirit of the New Left has, indeed, quite a lot in common with the celebrated Christian parable of the Good Samaritan.[91] Either way, it is beyond doubt that the activists of the New Left today have shaken the conscience of contemporary man out of its complacent satisfaction with the "bourgeois, individualist life" and stirred a large number of people into active participation. Seen in this light, the activities of the New Left would seem to be something entirely to be welcomed.

There is a problem here, however. The New Left stresses "solidarity" to the point where there is a real danger that the independent values of the individual will be lost sight of. Although it is true that the individual only acquires value through relating to others, and is obliged to seek solidarity if only for his own salvation, one begins to suspect that the sense of guilt that spurs on the New Left, and which they often summon up in others, is somehow lacking in depth. Their sense of guilt readily disappears, or at least is modified to a great extent, by that sense of solidarity, until it seems to lose its importance, at least for the person concerned.

This point is clear if one examines the theories of self-negation so strenuously preached at one stage by the students and teachers of Zenkyōtō—their idea that one should become aware of one's own guilt and "shed one's privileges." It is very doubtful whether one's "privileges" can in fact be shed completely, but observation suggests that where the individual succeeds in achieving some fellow-feeling with the person regarded as his victim, he becomes convinced that, in the process, this shedding has been achieved. Thus denial of the self becomes denial in the psychoanalytic sense. It is as though the questions within the individual had been resolved through fellowship with others.

I cannot help feeling that the sense of guilt touched off mainly by this kind of fellow feeling is extremely close to the sense of guilt peculiar to the Japanese that has been described earlier. Japanese often resign out of a sense of shared responsibility for some unfortunate incident, even where they have no personal responsibility, since not to do so would incur a sense of guilt at not having closed their ranks. The guilt of which the New Left talks is surely essentially similar, a more generalized version of the same thing. In the passage just quoted Oda Makoto says that "his Japan" is not the Japanese nation or the Japanese people in the narrow sense, but "a set of ties that stretch out to the world as a whole"—an idea which is surely more Japanese than even he realizes.

To sum up the preceding, let us compare once more the spirit of the New Left and the idea behind the parable of the Good Samaritan. The activists of the New Left admit that they too, like the priest and the Levite in the parable, have a lurking desire to pretend not to see the victim. In their analysis, this is the same as arraying oneself with the guilty, and means taking refuge in one's own privileged existence. So far, this agrees completely with the spirit of the parable; the trouble lies in what follows. They promptly resort to the logic of negation and deny their own privileges—but it does not follow that

161

they also take actual steps to aid the victim as the Good Samaritan did. On they contrary, they identify themselves with the victim; or, more accurately, the identification occurs simultaneously with the self-denial, since it is through identifying with the victim that they deny their own individual existence and thus, it seems, deny their sense of guilt. In this sense they become victims themselves and begin to abuse those who ignore the victim or, more positively, attack those responsible. The more unnatural the denial of the self that provides the starting-point, the more bellicose and violence-prone will be the action that stems from it.

Now this kind of sense of victimization can be seen as harboring a doubly convoluted *amae* mentality, since not only does the sense of being victimized derive, as we have seen, from unsatisfied *amae*, but here it is deliberately chosen for the sake of achieving a sense of community with others. The frame of mind of the victim is painful in itself, but the sense of being victimized that is chosen of one's own accord for the sake of the sense of community is relatively painless. The owner of such a sense of grievance, despite his victim mentality —or rather because of it—feels free to inflict harm on others, and even comes to experience a sadistic self-satisfaction in doing so. I hasten to add that I am not asserting that all attacks on or criticism of those who victimize others are wrong. The trouble starts when the attacks or criticism serve to get rid of one's own sense of guilt. This kind of guilt derives from *amae* and is typically facile; it is not the kind of guilt, discussed at the end of the preceding section, that serves as a basis for morality. The attack on injustice made out of concealed motives such as this can never be effective, but is more likely, on the contrary, to aid in its proliferation.

The century of the child

To say that the present age is strangely permeated with *amae* is much the same as saying that everyone has become more childish. Or it might be more correct to say that the distinction between children and adults has become blurred. Thanks to the mass communication media, children get to know things so quickly that an increasing number of them are too "adult" to consider their elders as adults. Indeed, although people talk of the generation "gap" it might be more appropriate as a description of the present to talk of the loss of any boundary between the generations. It is the same with adults: the "adult adult" of the past has disappeared and the number of childish adults has increased. And the element common to both adult-like child and childlike adult is *amae*.

A good illustration of this is seen in an article entitled "The Reluctant Adults" that appeared in the *Mainichi Shimbun* of August 22, 1970. Recently, it points out, the term *kakko ii* (smart, nice, "groovy") is being corrupted to *katcho ii*—the pronunciation of the child whose tongue cannot yet manage the correct sounds. Traditionally, youth is supposed to be a period when the individual is eager to become an adult and afraid of being looked down on as a child, but nowadays, it seems, youth is reluctant to grow up. The author says that he asked some young people what attracted them about long hair and flamboyant clothes, and was told that "it made one look cute." The desire to look cute is, as hardly needs pointing out, a typical expression of *amae*.

It is interesting that this trend should be found all over the world today and not only in Japan, long known as a "paradise for children." The increasing number of children who get killed by their parents nowadays in Japan might suggest that

163

it is not such a paradise after all, but if so the real reason is the increase in the number of childish parents—which is admirable proof that you cannot create a paradise for children without adults too. It may well be that, originally at least, the feeling of parents for their children was particularly strong in Japan. As early as the Nara period Yamanoue no Okura wrote a verse as he lay gravely ill in which he said that though he knew he must die the sight of his children made it difficult for him to accept death. On this score, probably, Japan was in advance of the West. Until the middle ages in the West, and even later among the lower classes, children were apparently left more or less to fend for themselves, and even later, when parents began to give thought to their children's education, it was the custom to separate them from their parents at an early age and send them to boarding school, where discipline was strict.[92] It is only very recently, it seems, that parents began to spoil their children in the Japanese sense (the well-known works of Dr. Spock are probably highly significant here). The Western sensibility where children are concerned has been drawing closer to the Japanese in recent years; but parallel with this there has been an increase in the number of children who never grow up. The scholars who see world history as a history of progress often claim that up till now man has been passing through his "infancy," in which all kinds of religious systems were imposed upon him, but that now those inhibitions have been removed and he has entered upon true adulthood for the first time. This is self-deception. The present seems just the reverse of an adult age. Moreover, while it may be not a bad thing for the adult, like the child, not to be bound by the past, it is not good for adults, like children, to behave impulsively, as the fancy takes them. The "sexual freedom" so apparent today can be interpreted, psychologically speaking, as a pure manifestation of the infantile polymorphous perversion as Freud defined it.

This phenomenon of childishness is seen in its most acute form in the hippy cult. Not, of course, that the spiritual attitudes embodied in the hippie are restricted to him alone. They influence the whole of society, every generation and every class. For example, the psychology of *kakko ii* extends to the world of adults and not only that of children and adolescents. I heard recently that whereas conductors in the past were economic in their use of gesture and body movement, which existed not for their effect on the audience but solely as a means of conducting the music, many of today's conductors are just a part of the show. They are obliged to use the baton in a *kakko ii* way.

Whether this is a welcome trend or not I could not say—not that there is any sense in discussing the point, since today's actuality is what it is. Nor is it of much use to argue that it is due to the influence of television, since the real question is that of the meaning of this contemporary phenomenon. Many people feel, apparently, that it is a sign of the end of one age and the beginning of another. In practice, the present tendency to shelve all distinctions—of adult and child, male and female, cultured and uncultured, East and West—in favor of a uniform childish *amae* can only be called a regression for mankind, yet it may prove to be a necessary step towards the creation of a new culture of the future, since it is recognized that in the individual the creative act is preceded by a kind of regressive phenomenon.[93] This assumes of course that humanity does have a future, which is something that no one can predict with certainty; many scholars, alarmed by the rapid progress of environmental contamination, are doubtful. No one can say whether this regressive phenomenon in mankind is a mortal sickness or a prelude to a new burst of good health. It is precisely in this unpredictability that the seriousness of our situation today lies.

165

6 *Amae* reconsidered

The wide attention attracted by the first edition of this book induced a gratifyingly large number of people to give thought to the question of *amae*. My own views too have been subject to much scrutiny, and occasionally to quite sharp criticism. I have already written two pieces in an attempt to reply to some of them,[94] but finding them still inadequate I decided to add some notes on what I feel. It is impossible, of course, to deal with all the criticisms individually; these are merely the second thoughts to which they have spurred me. [This chapter was written in 1981. *Ed.*]

The definition of *amae*

Although in this work I discuss the psychology of *amae* from a variety of viewpoints, my failure to relate it to ordinary psychological terms such as emotion, drive, or instinct seems to have somewhat perplexed people used to this kind of terminology. What, exactly—they want to know—is *amae*: is it an emotion, or a drive, or an instinct? I have touched briefly on this point in another, specialist work,[95] but to state my view briefly in relation to the criticisms made of the present book, I would say that *amae* is, first and foremost, an emotion, an emotion which partakes of the nature of a drive and with something instinctive at its base.

166

In order to explain this in somewhat more detail, let us assume that observation has produced the statement that a certain person is indulging in *amae*. The *amae* here indicates, first of all, an observed behavior: an overfamiliar attitude, for example, or a way of speaking designed to attract attention. However, the word, it would seem, really refers not to the observed behavior as such but to the emotion of which it is a sign. In considering the nature of this emotion, one must first of all examine the nature of what are referred to as emotions in general. Whether they involve pleasure or anger, grief or happiness, the thing they have in common, it seems, is that they all demonstrate a relationship between the one who feels the emotion and his surroundings. What kind of relationship, then, does the word *amae* suggest?

In its most characteristic form, it represents an attempt to draw close to the other person. This is why in the section on the psychological prototype of *amae* I defined *amae* as being, in the first place, the craving of a newborn child for close contact with its mother, and, in the broader sense, the desire to deny the fact of separation that is an inevitable part of human existence, and to obliterate the pain that this separation involves.

Dr. Kimura Bin, however, quotes the definitions given in the Japanese dictionaries *Daigenkai* and *Kōjien* in order to raise doubts concerning this interpretation of mine. Let us glance, then, at the relevant quotations. In *Daigenkai*, *amayu* (the literary form of the verb *amaeru*) is defined basically as "to depend on another's affection," while *amaeru* is described as "self-indulgent behavior by an infant of either sex presuming on the love of its parents." *Kōjien*, next, lists under *amayu*: "(1) to possess sweetness; (2) to presume on familiarity in order to 'make up to' the other, or to presume on familiarity in order to behave in a self-indulgent manner; (3) to feel awkward from a sense of shame, to be embarrassed." I also checked with a

167

few other dictionaries, but their definitions were much the same as those already quoted.

Dr. Kimura takes these definitions as a basis for claiming that *amae* is "not a word indicating a drive to dependence, seeking assimilation with the other" in the sense in which I explain it, but signifying "willful behavior in a situation in which one has, as it were, already been accepted and assimilation has taken place, or based on the self-indulgent assumption that permission on these lines has already been given." Dr. Kimura here uses a phrase, "a drive to dependence," which I do not use in this book, but this is because the specialist work mentioned above postulates a drive to dependence as the instinctive element underlying *amae*. I intend to leave this question aside here; but if Dr. Kimura is suggesting that the emotion of *amae* contains nothing in the way of a drive, I would object. If "drive" is too abstract, then "desire" will do as well, since, as I have suggested already, the feeling of *amae* indicates an urge to draw closer to another person, and in that sense it can be called a desire.

If, however, Dr. Kimura in the passage quoted is asserting that *amae* is an emotion that takes the other person's love for granted, an emotion that arises when assimilation is permitted, then I have no argument with him, since this is what I have said all along. *Amae*, in short, can only exist when *amae* is permitted. This may sound obvious; what cannot be dismissed as obvious is that the word *amae* is peculiar to Japan, and that the Japanese are particularly familiar with the emotion it represents. It would be no exaggeration to say that my whole theory of the Japanese evolved around this point. Accordingly, if this alleged truth is not in fact true, then my theories presumably amount to empty speculation. It did not even occur to me, I might add, to carry out any strict comparative study in order to corroborate this "truth."

The next point—the one, in fact, which has caused most

confusion among scholars—is that while my whole argument depends on the assertion that *amae* is a peculiarly Japanese emotion, I also assert that it has universal relevance. I make this claim because at the root of *amae* feelings there seems to lie something instinctive common to all mankind, the thing that I have labeled "the drive to dependence." This, some feel, involves a logical contradiction, since it means claiming a particular development for *amae* among the Japanese even though *amae*, if rooted in something instinctive, ought to be equally detectable in all human beings. There are two keys to this apparent contradiction. The first is that whereas in Japan human relations of a dependent nature are worked into the social norm, in the West they are excluded, with the result that *amae* developed in the former and not in the latter. The second, which does not necessarily contradict the first, is that even in Western societies where there is no convenient word corresponding to *amae* and feelings of *amae* would seem not to exist, a surprising amount of a similar kind of feeling can be observed if one looks at the phenomenon with Japanese eyes.

This last point is not the same as saying that where the feeling of *amae* does not exist there are substitutes for it. In the states referred to in Japanese as *uramu* (resenting) or *hinekureru* (being twisted), for example, one may say that while the emotion of *amae* as such is not present, there is a hidden wish to *amaeru*. Thus even when *amae* is not present as an emotion, it can exist in a different form. The script of a recent television drama included the remark: "He goes on cursing and swearing, but in fact it's just *amaeru*-ing." It seems safe to say that this use of *amaeru* is fairly widespread. *Amae* here is not an experienced emotion, but a hidden wish: a narcissistic *amae*, if you like. In the same way, one may say that *amae* exists even in Western society where it is not apprehended consciously as such. At various points in this work, I have made use of this logic without stating it explicitly, and I must apologize for the mental distress this has occasioned my more fastidious colleagues.

What I really want to discuss here, though, is my assertion that something that can clearly be labeled as an *emotion* of *amae*—and not just unrealized, unconscious *amae*—is to be found in Western society also. I have long been inclined to a positive view here, but not being in close touch with the typical Westerner's everyday life, I was unable to make the assertion with any degree of confidence. Subsequently, however, a number of foreign scholars have affirmed the existence of *amae* feelings in Western society, and I am sure they are to be relied on. Professor Rivera, in whom I have particular trust, has written that "once one becomes sensitive to *amae* one sees it evidenced in all kinds of behavior (e.g., the American male's imperious 'When is dinner going to be ready?'). But does it exist as a specific feeling—as an emotion? I believe that it does but is often masked under the general rubric of 'love.'... In short, I believe that it is precisely the emotion that is concerned with having the other belong to one and which I, lacking the term *amae*, had to label 'desire.' (In fact, probably *amae* is often a component of sexual desire or longing.)"[96]

I should like, finally, to cite an example of an *amae* emotion that occurred in a short story published in *The New Yorker*.[97] The hero, a corporate lawyer of thirty-five named Charles, has been divorced for a year. His ex-wife, Barbara, who lives with their daughter some six miles away, is—Charles declares—still his best friend, and he talks with her over the phone two or three times a week. Recently, however, she has begun to complain that she has lost her respect for him because he can't control his emotions. Having told her about his new girl friend, he keeps asking Barbara what he should do about her. The conversation invariably ends with his choking up, and Barbara telling him that if he can't control his emotions she'll hang up on him.

Now, the emotion that Charles is feeling in this sad little

story is, almost undoubtedly, *amae*. Since, however, he has no such word in his vocabulary, he can hardly apprehend it as such. Much less can Barbara recognize it as a particular emotion; she can only see it as a loss of emotional control.

This particular incident happens to be fiction, but there must be any number of such cases in actual society. I should make it clear here that I have not verified this through surveys. What I am trying to show through such examples, however, is that the existence of the feeling of *amae* is possible even in societies where there is no word to indicate it. It is, nonetheless, the existence or nonexistence of the word that makes all the difference. It was precisely to point out this fact that this book was written.

In passing, I would like to note that after writing the preceding, I read a paper sent to me by Professor Gerhard Schepers of International Christian University in Tokyo ("Images of *Amae* in Kafka—with special reference to *Metamorphosis*" *Humanities, Christianity and Culture*, ICU Publication IV-B, 15 July, 1980). Schepers quotes from Kafka's letters and works to argue convincingly that the emotional world of Kafka is one of *amae* —though I might add that the *amae* here, of course, is one that cannot be satisfied.

I also happened to see a movie by Bergman, *Scenes from a Marriage*, which was broadcast in six parts on Japanese television. This work, I felt, had much in it to suggest the presence of *amae*. In the last scene in particular, the wife has a nightmare in which for the first time she makes the terrifying discovery that "she has loved no one and been loved by no one." At this point, she is a typical example of a narcissism in which a natural manifestation of *amae* is blocked. What is particularly interesting, moreover, is that in this drama Bergman seems to be condemning contemporary Western civilization for giving rise to this kind of relationship between the sexes.

Amae and identification

If, as I have claimed, the feeling of *amae*, though finding particularly fertile soil in Japan, has in fact a universal relevance, then something corresponding to it ought surely to have attracted notice in Western psychology in the past. With this idea in mind, I have for some time been on the lookout for evidence of this, especially in the field of psychoanalysis, and have already mentioned one or two of my findings in this work —in relation, for example, to Freud's special views on homosexuality and to Balint's concept of passive object love. Comparatively recently, however, it dawned on me that Freud's concept of identification does in fact correspond to *amae*. For a long time, I failed to realize that these two things were one and the same, one reason being that *amae* is an everyday word indicating an experienced emotion, whereas identification is a scientific term adopted by Freud to indicate a wider psychological process. Even so, I did have a vague feeling that there was a close connection between the two: if *amae* was an emotion arising when the desire to depend was satisfied, I reasoned, then identification was possibly something that arose when it was *not* satisfied.[98] The hint for this came from Freud's own accounts of identification, but I still felt that something was unsatisfactory; for one thing, it was not clear just how *amae* fitted into the framework of traditional psychoanalytical theory, nor was I completely clear in my mind about the concept of identification as such.

Dr. Ohashi Hideo recently published an extremely perceptive paper on these subjects, which I recommend to anyone interested.[99] Here I will pursue the argument further only insofar as it is relevant to the main theme of this book. It seems likely that Freud was, ultimately, seeking to describe what we think of when we hear the word *amae*, since he remarks that "identification is, first of all, the original form of emotional tie with an object."[100] He was much troubled by the question of how to relate identification on the one hand with, on the other, the object choice which represented sexual love, and seems to have remained dissatisfied with his own explanations.[101] There is no need here to trace all the convolutions of his thought, though I personally suspect that part of his difficulty was a resistance to experiencing identification as an emotion, that is, as a feeling of *amae*.

An instance of a situation that becomes easier to explain when one assumes that identification and *amae* are the same occurs in the parent-child relationship. If the parent spoils the child, the latter, though it may seem to be *amaeru*-ing, in fact becomes incapable of doing so. The reason is that in such cases the one who does the spoiling is, in reality, "seeking to be spoiled" (*amaeru*). Though the truth of this may not be apparent without a degree of intuition, it is more readily understandable if one says that the one who is doing the spoiling is *identifying* with the other. In other words, the former is pre-empting the latter's attempt to identify. The latter cannot identify with the former, and thus cannot *amaeru*.

The individual and the group

One of my main preoccupations in this book, as most readers, I am sure, will have sensed, is with the question of the individual and the group. The Japanese are often said to be group-minded, to be strong as a group but weak as individuals. It is also said that the freedom of the individual is still not firmly established in Japanese society. Where general trends are concerned, these statements would seem to be true, and they accord well with the prominence of *amae* in Japanese society.

To use a term discussed above, the Japanese are good at identification. In short, by becoming one with the group the Japanese are able to display a strength beyond the scope of the individual.

The point that arises here is that this typically Japanese characteristic is often negatively evaluated. Considered carefully, however, there is surely nothing particularly bad about it in itself. Without some kind of group life, it is doubtful in fact whether man could survive at all. One proof of this is seen in the mentally disturbed patient, whose misfortune is a result of isolation consequent on his failure in some way or other to adjust to group life. Even the West with its well-known freedom of the individual has its own forms of group life; indeed, the mental patient in the West can be said to be a failure within the group in just the same way as his counterpart in Japan. In the West, too, this means the group plays a part in sustaining the individual. A passage that I happened to read in Bernard Crick's *In Defence of Politics* further opened my eyes in this direction.[102] Criticizing the political ideas of Jean-Jacques Rousseau, who sought on principle to deny the existence of any subsidiary group within the State, he says: "For rights to have any meaning they must adhere to particular institutions: the rights of Englishmen are, indeed, necessarily more secure than the Rights of Man."

This made me wonder once more just what was the true nature of individual freedom in the West, and why it should be difficult in Japan for the individual to throw off the pressure of the group. The answer, I feel, is hinted at in a study of the group by Georg Simmel.[103] As he sees it, "the medieval group in the strict sense [in Europe] was one which did not permit the individual to become a member in other groups....The modern type of group-formation makes it possible for the isolated individual to become a member in whatever number of groups he chooses." It is in these terms that he sees the individualism of modern Europe, and his view has led me to conclude that the Japanese failure so far to develop individual freedom in the Western sense is either because the group, as I have suggested in this book, was constructed in concentric circles, or because groups merely existed side by side, like a household of many different families, without any interpenetration. "Freedom of the individual" does not mean that the individual is free in himself, as he is; freedom is only acquired through the fact of participation in another group originally unrelated to the group to which he belongs. And I suspect that the potential for this type of cross-movement existed in Western history and culture from the beginning and not, as Simmel says, in modern times only.

References

1. Benedict, R. *The Chrysanthemum and the Sword*, Tuttle, Tokyo, 1954.
2. Doi, L. T. "Some Aspects of Japanese Psychiatry" *Am J. Psychiat.*, III: 691–695, 1955.
3. Doi, L. T. "Japanese Language as an Expression of Japanese Psychology" *Western Speech*, Spring, 1956.
4. Doi, L. T. "Amaeru koto" *Aiiku Shinri*, Vol. 75, Feb. 1956.
5. Doi, L. T. "Shinkeishitsu no seishin byōri—toku ni toraware no seishin rikigaku ni tsuite," *Seishin Shinkeishi*, Vol. 60, VII 633–744, 1958.
6. Doi, L. T. "Jibun to amae no seishin byōri" *Seishin shinkeishi*, Vol. 62, I 149–162 1960.
7. Freud, S. "Contributions to the Psychology of Love—the Most Prevalent Form of Degradation in Erotic Life," *Collected Papers* 4, Basic, New York.
8. Balint, Michael. *Primary Love and Psychoanalytic Technique*. Liveright, New York, 1965.
9. Doi, L. T. "Amae—a Key Concept for Understanding Japanese Personality Structure," *Japanese Culture*: *Its Development and Characteristics* (Smith, R. J., and Beardsley, R. K., eds.) Aldine, Chicago, 1962.
10. Nakamura, H. *Tōyōjin no shii hōhō 3*, Shunjūsha, Tokyo, 1962.
11. Doi, L. T. "Some Thoughts on Helplessness and the Desire to be loved," *Psychiatry* 26, 266–272, 1963.
12. Freud, S. *Future of an Illusion*, Liveright, New York.
13. Doi, L. T. "Giri-Ninjō: An Interpretation" *Aspects of Social Change in Modern Japan*, ed. by R. P. Dore. Princeton University Press, New Jersey, 1967.
14. Maruyama, M. *Nippon no shisō*, Iwanami shinsho, Tokyo, 1961.

15. Doi, L. T. *Seishin Bunseki*, Kyōritsu Shuppansha, Tokyo, 1956.
16. Doi, L. T. *Seishin Bunseki to Seishin Byōri*, Igaku Shoin, Tokyo, 1965.
17. Doi, L. T. "Shinkeishō no Nipponteki Tokusei—Tsuika Toron" *Seishin Igaku* Vol. 6 II, pp. 119–123, 1964.
18. Doi, L. T. "Momotarō to Zengakuren" *Aiiku Shinri*, March, 1960.
19. Doi, L. T. "Tatakau Gendai Seinen no Shinri" *Nippon Keizai Shimbun*, Nov. 24, 1968.
20. Doi, L. T. "Kagaisha Ishiki to Higaisha Ishiki" *Hihyo*, Vol. 16 pp. 2–12 1969.
21. Nakane, C. *Japanese Society*, California Press, Berkeley, 1972.
22. Dore, R. P. *City Life in Japan*, Routledge & Kegan Paul, London, 1958.
23. Yanagida, K. *Mainichi no Kotoba*, Sōgen Bunko, Tokyo, 1951.
24. Minamoto, R. *Giri to Ninjō—Nipponteki Shinjō no Ichi Kōsatsu*, Chūō Shinsho, Tokyo, 1969.
25. Satō, T. *Seiji Ishiki to Seikatsu Kankaku*, Chikuma Shobō, Tokyo, 1960.
26. Nakamura, H. see reference 10, above.
27. Hearn, L. *Kokoro*; *Hints and echoes of Japanese life*, Reprint Hse Intl, New York.
28. Xavier, St. Francis. *Shokansho*, Vol. 2, Iwanami Bunko, Tokyo, 1949.
29. Lu Hsun. *Three stories by Lu Hsun*, Cambridge U. Pr., New York.
30. Doi, L. T. "Seishin Bunseki to Nipponteki Seikaku, *Shisō*, Nov. 1969 Iwanami Shoten.
31. Heuvers, H. "Shikararete" *Jinsei no Aki ni*, Shunjūsha, Tokyo, 1969.
32. Ishida, E. *Nippon Bunka Ron*, Chikuma Shobō, Tokyo, 1969.
33. Hearn, L. see reference 27, above.
34. Aristoteles. *Nichomachean Ethics*, Harvard, Cambridge Mass.
35. Erikson, Erik H. *Childhood and Society*, p. 252. Norton, New York, 1963.
36. Lynd, Helen M. *On Shame and the Search for Identity*, Harvard, Cambridge, Mass.
37. Bonhoeffer, Dietrich. *Ethics*. Macmillan, New York, 1964.
38. Sakuta, K. *Haji no Bunka Saikō*, Chikuma Shobō, Tokyo, 1967.
39. Maruyama, M. see reference 14, above.
40. Sapir, Edward *Language*, Harvard, Cambridge, Mass., 1949.

41. Cassirer, Ernst. *An Essay on Man*, Doubleday, New York, 1954.
42. Whorf, Benjamin L. *Language, Thought, and Reality*, p. 252. M.I.T. Cambridge, Mass., 1956.
43. Freud, S. *An Outline of Psychoanalysis*, p. 41. Norton, New York, 1949.
44. Rapaport, D. "The Conceptual Model of Psychoanalysis" *Psychoanalytic Psychiatry and Psychology*, ed. Robert P. Knight and Cyrus R. Friedman, International Universities Press, New York, 1954.
45. Kubie, S. L. *Practical and Theoretical aspects of Psychoanalysis*, Intl. Univ. Pr., New York.
46. Kubie, S. L. "The Distortion of the Symbolic Process in Neurosis and Psychosis" *J. Amer Psychoanal. Asso.*, 1, 59–86, 1953.
47. Langer, S. K. "Emotion and Abstraction" *Philosophical Sketches*, Mentor, New York, 1964.
48. Izumi, S. Inoue, M. Umesao, T. "Nippon Jin to Nippon teki Shikō" (round table talk), *Tosho*, May 1970, Iwanami Shoten.
49. Nakamura, H. see reference 10, above.
50. Mori, A. "Nippon no Shisō, Chūgoku no Shisō, Seiyō no Shisō" (round table talk with Yoshikawa, K. and Bido, M.) *Tosho*, Sept., 1970, Iwanami Shoten.
51. Suzuki, D. "Tōyō Bunmei no Kontei ni aru Mono" *Asahi Shimbun*, Dec. 22, 1958.
52. Maruyama, M. see reference 14, above.
53. Motoori, N. *Suzuya Tōmon Roku*, Iwanami Bunko, Tokyo.
54. Kuki, S. *Iki no Kōzō*, Iwanami Shoten, Tokyo, 1967.
55. Nishida, K. *Zen no Kenkyū*, Iwanami Bunko, Tokyo.
56. Tsuda, S. "Jiyū to yū Go no Yōrei" *Shisō, Bungei, Nippon Go*, Iwanami Shoten, 1956.
57. Zilboorg, Gregory. *A History of Medical Psychology*, Norton, New York, 1941.
58. Herbert, George. *Outlandish Proverbs*, Hotten, London, 1874.
59. Sidney, Algernon. *Discourses Concerning Government*, Littlebury, London, 1698.
60. Doi, L. T. *Sōseki no Shinteki Sekai*, cf Chapter 2, Shibundō, Tokyo, 1969.
61. *New Testament*, St. Paul, Galatea Chapter 5.
62. Luther, M. *Christian Liberty*, Fortress, Philadelphia.
63. Troeltsch, Ernst. *Christian Thought: its History and Application*, (1923) p. 120–121. Meridian, New York, 1957.

64. Morita, S. *Shinkeishitsu no Hontai to Ryōhō*, p. 29, Hakuyōsha, Tokyo, 1955.
65. Ladee, G. A. *Hypochondriacal Syndromes*, Elsevier, New York, 1966.
66. Schulte, W. *Studien zur heutigen Psychotherapie*, Quelle und Meyer, Heidelberg, 1954.
67. *Seishin Bunseki Kenkyū*, Vol. 15, II, 1969 Symposium, cf. "Hitomishiri".
68. Spitz, R. *The First Year of Life*, Intl. Univ. Pr., New York, 1965.
69. Tönnies, F. *Community and Society*, Mich. St. U. Pr., Ann Arbor.
70. Nishida, H. "Seinenki Shinkeishō no Jidaiteki Hensen," *Jidō Seishin Igaku to sono Kinsetsu Ryōiki*, Vol. 9 p. 225, 1968.
71. Doi, L. T. *Sōseki no Shinteki Sekai*, cf Chapter 9, Shibundō, 1969.
72. Freud S. "Mourning and Melancholia " *Collected Papers* 4, Basic, New York.
73. Satō, T. "Hadaka no Nippon Jin," *Nippon Jin no Kokoro* (Gendai no Esprit), Shibundō, 1965.
74. Kierkegaard, S. *The Present Age*, Har Row, New York.
75. Scheler, M. *Ressentiment*, Free Pr., New York.
76. Kindaichi H. "Nippon Go no Tokushoku to wa" *Kotoba no Kenkyūshitsu*, Nippon Hōsō Kyōkai, 1954.
77. Doi, L. T. "Jama no Shinri ni Tsuite" *Ima ni Ikiru*, 32nd issue, April, 1969.
78. Maruyama, M. see reference 14, above.
79. Doi, L. T. *Seishin Bunseki to Seishin Byōri* (revised edition 1970), (see reference 16, above).
80. Kant, I. Anthropology from a Pragmatical Point of View.
81. Ortega y Gasset. *Man and Crisis*, Norton, New York, 1962.
82. Lidz, Theodore. *The Family and Human Adaptation*, Intl. Univ. Pr., New York, 1963.
83. Lifton, R. J. *History and Human Survival*, Chapter 1. Random, New York, 1970.
84. Federn, P. "On the Psychology of Revolution; the Fatherless Society." *Der Aufstieg*, *Neue Zeit-und Streitschriften*, 1919, 12–13, Vienna: Anzenbruber, 29 pp. (Quoted in: "Psychoanalysis and Education—an Historical Account," R. Ekstein and R. L. Motto, *The Reiss-Davis Clinic Bulletin*, Vol. 1, No. 1, 1964).
85. Freud, S. *Totem and Taboo* and *Moses and Monotheism*, Random, New York, 1955.
86. Doi, L. T. "Freud no Isan" *Seiki*, May 1967.
87. Marcuse, H. *Eros and Civilization*, Random, New York, 1955.

88. Nietzsche, F. *Joyful Wisdom*, Ungan, New York.

89. Grunberger, Béla and Smirgel, J. C. *L'Univers Contestationnair ou les Nouveaux Chrétiens—Etude Psychanalytique*, Payot, Paris.

90. Oda, M. "Watakushi no naka no Nippon Jin" (4) *Asahi Shimbun*, March 18, 1969.

91. *New Testament*, St Luke, Chapter 10.

92. Aries, Philippe. *Centuries of Childhood—A Social History of Family Life* Knopf, New York, 1962.

93. Kris, E. "On Preconscious Mental Processes" *Psy. Quart.*, 19, 540–560, 1950.

94. Doi, L. T. "Amae no kōzō hoi" *Amae Zakkō*, Kōbundō, Tokyo, 1975.

——"Amae ni tsuite ni dai" *Loisir*, May 1977. Leisure Development Center, Tokyo.

95. Doi, L. T. *Seishin Bunseki to Seishin Byōri*, pp. 45–48. Igaku Shoin, 1970.

96. Rivera, Joseph de. *A Structural Theory of the Emotions* p. 127. Intl. Univ. Pr., New York, 1977.

97. Falsey, John. "Bachelors" *The New Yorker*, January 9, 1978.

98. Doi, L. T. *Seishin Bunseki to Seishin Byōri*, p. 98. Igaku Shoin, 1970.

99. Ohashi, H. "Amae no benshōhō" *Rinshō Seishin Igaku Ronshū*, Seiwa Shoten, Tokyo, 1980.

100. Freud, S. *Complete Psychological Works* (Standard Edition), Vol. 18, p. 107. (Group Psychology and Analysis of the Ego), Hogarth Pr., London, 1971.

101. Freud, S. *Complete Psychological Works* (Standard Edition), Vol. 22, p. 63. (New Introductory Lectures on Psychoanalysis).

102. Crick, Bernard. *In Defence of Politics* pp. 47–48. Penguin, 1964.

103. Simmel, Georg. *Conflict and the Web of Group Affiliations*, Free Pr., New York, 1955.